HAUNTED NORTHERN VIRGINIA

ALEX MATSUO

Haunted America

Published by Haunted America
A Division of The History Press
Charleston, SC
www.historypress.com

First published 2024

Manufactured in the United States

ISBN 9781467156554

Library of Congress Control Number: 2024937577

Dedicated to those who perceive the world through a spiritual lens, patiently attuned to the untold tales of our past.

CONTENTS

PREFACE

It wasn't until I relocated to Northern Virginia (NOVA) that I realized what a truly unique area this is compared to the rest of the state. In fact, I would argue that NOVA could easily become a state of its own and the rest of Virginia wouldn't notice the difference. The stark contrast is so severe that it's immediately noticeable once you drive down I-95 South. But this is part of what makes Northern Virginia a truly unique place. It makes the state a contradiction of itself, between rural and city life, rich and poor, urban and suburban and historical versus modern development. The latter is probably one of the most important factors when considering NOVA's push for modernization while the past is crying out to be heard.

When I first moved to Arlington in January 2022, I conducted an assessment of haunted locations as a way to connect with this new community and learn more about the area. Being a paranormal investigator, I'm always scoping out new locations to research and explore. I was shocked when I realized that NOVA is a gold mine of haunted locations. And yet they're not as well-known as other haunted areas in the rest of the state. Why is this?

I wanted to dig deeper because many of these haunted locations are rooted in rich history that is well acknowledged. But uttering the words *ghosts* and *spirits* brings about silence and eagerness to change the subject.

Haunted history is history, and the spirits of historical figures could potentially be available to talk to us directly, which is what I love most about haunted history. Plus, we have an amazing opportunity to spend time in these historic locations in a way that goes beyond conventional tourism.

This book is a love letter to the people of Northern Virginia who are eager to have their voices heard—many of whom only exist now in ghost stories, and these ghost stories keep their name immortal. Writing this book has given me the incredible opportunity to take a pulse on some of the most haunted places in Northern Virginia, some of which are a short drive away from Washington, D.C.

The history of Northern Virginia is a complicated mix of the aftermath of the Revolutionary War as well as the Civil War. When it comes to the latter, many of the ghost stories are tied to Confederate soldiers. Virginia did secede with the Confederacy, and that history cannot be sugarcoated. Ghost stories could be interpreted as sugarcoating; they act as a buffer, softening the harsh blow of the reality of what took place during various parts of U.S. history. In no way does this book condone the actions of the Confederates or the horrific practice that was slavery.

Simply put, this book shares ghost stories and the cultural history associated with them with respect and reverence. Some of the sites in this book are former plantations, which have their own share of horrific trauma toward enslaved people—more specifically, Black Americans.

Colin Dickey theorizes in his book *Ghostland: An American History in Haunted Places* that ghost stories can be a way for people to cope with the most difficult chapters of U.S. history. This is a reflection of the discomfort and anxiety of modern-day people trying to make sense of the actions of the past. Some believe that we need to prioritize the stories of the living and not soften the trauma with ghost stories. This is not for me to decide for you; I can only bring awareness of this possibility.

The public is taking a new interest in historical locations thanks to ghost stories, and people who may not have been interested before are part of the reason why ghost tours—which have become a meaningful way to make money—sell out. In this book, I prioritize the stories of haunted places and what remains from past trauma so that we can learn more, respect the experiences of the people who lived here before us and acknowledge their existence.

It's important to note that the information provided represents the best of my findings, and any errors are solely mine. Along with consulting books, websites, magazines and newspapers, I had the pleasure of interviewing several people for information. I had the honor of visiting most of the locations in this book—except a select few I wasn't able to, due to the fact that the location is now private property or it isn't standing anymore. I do advise that if you decide to visit these locations, respect their business hours and visiting policies. Also, try not to be disruptive, especially if you're visiting a hotel or a restaurant, so that you don't creating a tense environment for the patrons trying to enjoy the location. Finally, have fun and say hello to the spirits of these locations, whether verbally or in your mind. I'm sure the ghosts will appreciate the friendly hello.

ACKNOWLEDGEMENTS

This book would not have been possible without the assistance of the following people and organizations:

John Stanton and Heather Crocetto of the Arlington Center for Local History with the Arlington Public Library

Vayne Konstantine of Occoquan, Virginia

Peter Kelpinski

Loudoun Museum

Purcellville Library

Dana Henchen of the Loudoun County Library

Ann Carneal of the Thomas Balch Library

Fairfax Library

Arlington Historical Society

Ang DiNardo, president of Mason's Folklore Roundtable

John Stanton from the Center of Local History in Arlington

Phil Rossi and Tee Morris of Old Spirits Investigations, for sharing their experiences and taking me out to several of these locations.

Phillipa Ballentine for her generosity in sharing with me her research notes on the Candy Factory/ARTFactory in Manassas.

My cats, Chloe, Zoe, Sophie, Towa and Cali (may she rest in peace), for sitting vigil with me while I wrote in the early mornings and late evenings.

My husband, Chris, for being my biggest cheerleader and bringing me iced green tea so I didn't have to stop writing to grab it myself.

Finally, I owe my thanks to you, dear reader, for investing in this book with your time and money. I know you have many books of ghost stories and haunted places around the Washington, D.C. area to choose from, and I'm grateful you're holding this one in your hands.

INTRODUCTION

The state of Virginia in its entirety is full of history, which includes trauma, torment, new opportunities and discovery. It was one of the first colonies in the United States. Colonists were attacked by Indigenous communities as they infiltrated the New World. The Revolutionary War saw many battles in Virginia, and during the Civil War, more battles and death occurred in the commonwealth than anywhere else. Not only that, but Virginians have also preserved homes from as far back as the 1700s.

But Northern Virginia is a different place than the rest of the state. Given its proximity to Washington, D.C.—an area known for not only politics but also its ghosts—Northern Virginia is very much in the shadows.

And yet, Northern Virginia is one of the most densely populated areas in the state, with some of the richest history in the Washington, D.C. metro area. There's Old Town Alexandria, Manassas, Fairfax, Arlington, Leesburg and more. All these areas played important roles in the history of the United States. When one ventures out of the most city-centric areas, there are battlefields, historic homes and legends that either keep one inside at night or tempt the curious to venture out beyond their comfort zone.

Scientists and spiritualists have been debating the existence of ghosts for centuries. If civilization were to find the answer, it could either derail the fabric of societal rules and standards or provide validation and peace about the great beyond. Regardless of how one feels about ghosts and whether you believe, there is still value in ghost stories.

People learn about the history of locations by exploring the ghost stories that surround them. While yes, it's great to look in the history books, diving deep into the ghost lore of a town can give one a unique perspective on the cultural beliefs of the past. Northern Virginia is an area where progress is being made rapidly, sometimes at the expense of its history. Given the area's proximity to Washington, D.C., and its significant value for the railroad system, it seemed to be a magnet for bloodshed during the Civil War.

Northern Virginia is also an area of constant transition, traffic jams, corporate office buildings, technology and more. What was once called the Northern Neck is now lovingly called Northern Virginia, or NOVA for short. Politicians, scientists, doctors—some of the best in the world—have made their home in the area. In the busyness of NOVA, standing still on the sidelines, are the ghosts of the past, watching as we drive by.

These ghosts have stories to tell. Are you willing to listen?

Part I

Across the River from D.C.

CHAPTER 1
ALEXANDRIA, VIRGINIA

Before colonization, Alexandria was home to at least two Indigenous tribes: the Tauxenents and the Nacotchtanks. They were both part of a larger affiliation known as the Conoy chiefdom. Thousands of Native Americans lived in the region and had done so for about thirteen thousand years. In 1608, John Smith met these tribes and recorded their presence. After Smith left, it would be several years before European settlers started making their way into the area. Alexandria was part of a six-thousand-acre land grant that was given by Sir William Berkeley, governor of Virginia, to English ship captain Robert Howson in 1669. King Charles II approved the land grant as a thank-you gift to Howson for bringing 120 people to Virginia. A few months later, John Alexander purchased the land from Howson for six thousand pounds of tobacco. European settlers wouldn't drive out the Indigenous communities until 1675.

Founded in 1749, Alexandria, Virginia, is a town that sits on the Potomac River. One of Alexandria's more frequent visitors was none other than the first president of the United States, George Washington. In fact, he would have his crops sent to the Alexandria Farmer's Market, which is one of the oldest farmer's markets in the country that still runs today.

Alexandria's economy was all about tobacco, and it was one of the most extensive trading posts in the area. Sadly, it was also home to one of the largest slave-trading firms prior to the Civil War.

During the War of 1812, Alexandria found itself on the receiving end of British cannons and muskets. The Americans were given the opportunity to either fight—or surrender and their town would be spared. Alexandria opted to surrender, which is likely why it still has the historic buildings it does today. However, this proved to be a humiliating act for Alexandria, and the papers condemned Alexandria's mayor and other leaders of the town for being cowards.

Over the years, historical societies and other organizations have actively worked to preserve Old Town Alexandria, and many of its old buildings are still standing. Given the town's vast history, the idea of ghosts lurking about its historic buildings is less than surprising.

THE BURNING BRIDE OF ALEXANDRIA

At the time this book was written, 107 N. Fairfax Street has a coffee and gelato shop on the ground floor and an AirBnB on the upper floors.

In June 1868, Laura M. Schafer lived with her family in this house. On the bottom floor was a confectionery run by her father, Christian Schafer, who was a prominent citizen of Alexandria. The Schafer family lived on the second and third floors.

One fateful night in late June, Laura was getting dressed for bed on the third floor. Her grandmother Mrs. Ballenger was in the room with her. According to an article in the *Alexandria Gazette*, Laura went to her father's room to say goodnight. She wasn't even halfway into her father's room when she heard the glass of her kerosene lamp crack. The burning oil from the lamp landed on Laura's dress, and she frantically threw the lamp into the hearth in her father's room and ran, screaming and crying for help. The wind from Laura's running only fanned the flames. By the time she reached the bottom floor, the flames had risen above her head. Her brother-in-law William Phillips had been on the stairs in front of the house when he heard her cries. Her mother tried to help her while Phillips removed his coat and wrapped Laura in it, extinguishing

Schafer House. *Author's collection.*

the flames. Laura's grandmother put out the flames in her father's room using a blanket.

Laura was badly burned—as the *Alexandria Gazette* described it, "to a crisp." By eleven o'clock the next morning, Laura had passed away, with her companion, Charles Tenneson, by her side.

It was rumored that Laura and Charles were engaged to be married, but this was never confirmed. They were friends for years, and Laura wouldn't take another man as a friend.

Charles took Laura's death hard. The day of her death, he started drinking. Charles's friend Henry Green walked with him to the local wholesale liquor store and bar. Green didn't have a key to the back door, so Charles waited for him in Ramsay Alley, which was right next to the Schafer House. Green let Charles in through the back door and offered to buy him a drink. After the two men said, "Cheers," Charles said, "Here's to you and I—God save us." As Green took his empty glass back to the bar, he heard a gunshot. The heartbroken Charles had put a pistol to his head. Initially unconscious, he passed away around 3:20 p.m.

Local churches took care of the final arrangements for the young pair. Laura is buried at Washington Street United Methodist Church in Alexandria, and it's believed that Charles is buried not too far from her.

The Schafer House went through a few different identities after it was with the Schafer family. It has been a real estate agency, a Christmas trinket store called the Christmas Attic and, once again, a candy store. According to Michael Lee Pope, author of *Ghosts of Alexandria*, tenants who have owned and worked in the building know something is different and not quite right.

One local ghost tour guide shared that she felt lightheaded and dizzy when she visited the house while it was the Christmas Attic. Employees of the business also shared that they would find Christmas trees and other holiday props had been knocked down when they opened the store in the morning.

When Candida Kreb opened Candi's Candies in the house in 2007, she didn't know the story of Laura Schafer—until a ghost tour stopped by outside the shop one evening. Kreb told the group that she didn't believe in ghosts before closing the second-story window. But then she had an experience that changed her mind.

Kreb was working alone one evening while closing the shop when she smelled something burning. She went to the hallway to search for the source but didn't find anything. Using her nose, Kreb followed the smell upstairs but, once again, found nothing. Kreb decided it must have been a neighbor smoking and closed the shop for the night. The next day, the smell came back. Kreb went to investigate once more, walking toward the same staircase that Laura ran down for her life—and it was then that she remembered the story of Laura.

This wouldn't be Kreb's only experience. One night, she was cleaning the store when she had an overwhelming feeling of being watched. She heard a voice in her head say, "Enough. Leave." Kreb didn't stick around; she quickly took the cash register and left. She believes this was Laura telling her that she overstayed her welcome and it was time to go. Kreb also reported feeling an overwhelming presence in the basement, which she described as male.

Kreb kept a receipt signed by Laura M. Schafer behind the cash register. It is unknown if the coffee and gelato shop still has it, but it's a nice reminder that there are real people behind these stories.

Variations of the story of Laura Schafer's tragic end and the paranormal experiences that followed have become widely popular. According to the story I heard on a ghost tour, Laura was a bride, and the wedding was taking place at the confectionery and in the town square right next door. Laura the bride was upstairs when the kerosene lamp broke and the burning oil spilled onto her wedding dress. Like the real story, Laura the bride ran downstairs, engulfed in flames. But this time, she ran outside to the wedding reception while ablaze in front of her wedding guests. Other variations state that Laura was trying on her wedding dress for the ceremony that would take place a week later. This is why Laura became known as the Burning Bride of Alexandria.

Similar deviations from the story have also affected Charles Tenneson's legacy, with some versions pinning his death in Ramsay Alley instead of the bar. Other variations of the story even have Charles as a stalker throwing stones at Laura's window and setting her on fire himself.

Given the horrific tragedy of Laura's death, no embellishments or exaggerations are needed. As long as there are people who are dedicated to sharing the true story of Laura's passing, her legacy can live on.

LEE-FENDALL HOUSE

The Lee-Fendall House was built in 1785 and it served as a home for thirty-seven members of the Lee family, a hospital during the Revolutionary War, a Civil War hospital for Union soldiers and a home for free and enslaved

Lee-Fendell House. *Author's collection.*

Black people. The apparitions spotted at the Lee-Fendall House include nameless women, sighted only in period clothing. A woman and child in period clothing have also been spotted on the back stairs.

There have been no reports of these ghostly women saying anything to those who see them. The house was featured on an episode of *Ghost Hunters*, meaning the sightings were common enough for it to be worthy of a visit. Are these women trapped within the house? Or is hanging back from the other side the only way they can experience liberation?

GADSBY'S TAVERN

Gadsby's Tavern is one of the most popular historic sites to visit in the Washington, D.C., and Northern Virginia area. Named after Englishman John Gadsby, the site includes two buildings: a tavern that opened in 1785 and a hotel known as the City Tavern that opened in 1792. Gadsby leased the buildings and ran them as tavern keeper from around 1796 until 1808. The tavern's extensive history includes several Birthnight Balls (public celebrations of George Washington's birthday) and visits from prominent figures such as George Washington, John Adams, Thomas Jefferson, James Monroe and James Madison.

Gadsby's Tavern. *Author's collection.*

On July 25, 1816, a ship known as *Four Sons* arrived on the Potomac River and dropped anchor in Alexandria. There, a man and his sick wife were sent ashore. The ship was heading to the West Indies from Nova Scotia, but it made a special stop to send away the man and sick wife. On arrival, the couple were sent to the City Hotel, also known as Gadsby's Tavern, and they checked into room 8. What was mysterious about the couple was that the woman wore a veil over her face, so no one could tell what she looked like.

The distraught husband hired a local doctor by the name of Samuel Richards to attend to his sick wife, but not much could be done. Other doctors were also called in, believed to have been hired under the condition that they not publicly identify the woman, who became known as the Female Stranger.

On October 14, 1816, the Female Stranger took her last breath in her husband's arms. The town truly came together for the widower, with a local merchant even loaning money to cover burial arrangements. The unidentified husband gave the merchant, Lawrence Hill, a note from the Bank of England, which turned out to be a forgery. The husband disappeared without a trace after his wife was buried.

The Female Stranger was laid to rest without a name in St. Paul's Cemetery in Alexandria. Six pillars hold up a tabletop-like slab with the following inscription:

To the memory of a
FEMALE STRANGER
whose mortal sufferings terminated
on the 14th day of October 1816
Aged 23 years and 8 months
This stone is placed here by her disconsolate
Husband in whose arms she sighed out her
latest breath, and who under God
did his utmost even to soothe the cold
dead ear of death
How loved how valued once avails thee not
To whom related or by whom begot
A heap of dust alone remains of thee
Tis all thou art and all the proud shall be
To him gave all the Prophets witness that
through his name whosoever believeth in
him shall receive remission of sins
Acts. 10th Chap. 43rd verse

Hill managed to track down the widower a few years later during a visit to Sing Sing prison in New York. This time, he was identified as having the last name Clermont.

Theories about the identity of the Female Stranger vary. One of the most popular is that the Female Stranger was Theodosia Burr Alston, daughter of Aaron Burr, who was lost at sea in 1813. This theory was validated by a rumored visit to the grave by Theodosia's husband, Governor Alston. It is also believed that the Female Stranger and her husband were star-crossed lovers, a daughter of nobility and a British officer who wanted to be together and had to run away to do so.

The ghost of the Female Stranger dominates not only the history of Gadsby's Tavern but also Old Town Alexandria. She is often seen from the street through the windowpanes, holding a candle. She has been seen wandering the hallways of Gadsby's Tavern and has even been glimpsed by the staff of the restaurant. When Gadsby's Tavern was owned by the American Legion, members reported seeing a shadowy figure in the halls that would quickly disappear. Not only that, but the Female Stranger has also been seen by her grave in St. Paul's Cemetery.

One of the most prominent sightings was in the ballroom during one of the many Birthnight Balls celebrating the birthday of George Washington, with people dressing up in eighteenth-century clothing, dancing to music from the era and eating Washington's favorite foods. The Female Stranger is said to have made an appearance, and she stuck out like a sore thumb because she was wearing clothes from the early nineteenth century. Variations of this story include the visit happening right around the time after the Female Stranger would have died. If this is legitimate, then the Birthnight Ball attendees of the nineteenth century would have seen a woman in what they would have considered to be modern clothing—not wearing period clothing from the eighteenth century, which would have been the dress code for the event.

Either way you look at it, the ghost of the Female Stranger is a nod to a time when Alexandria was recovering from embarrassment after quickly surrendering during the War of 1812.

What is also interesting is that despite the popularity of the Female Stranger, Gadsby's Tavern Museum doesn't mention her during its tour. The story of this mysterious woman lives on through oral tradition, ghost tours and writeups. Even though there's a physical landmark—her grave—to show that she existed in some form, perhaps the museum isn't quite ready to dive deeper into the more supernatural side of the building.

The Alexandrian

The Alexandrian is a hotel that sits at 480 King Street. Before it was known as the Alexandrian, it was the Hotel Monaco Alexandria. Yet the building was not the first at that property, which used to be the home of the Marshall House, established in 1749. The original building was torn down in the 1950s for the sake of urban development and modernization.

The history surrounding the haunting of the Marshall House dates to May 24, 1861. The day before, a public referendum was held to support Virginia's secession from the United States. Tensions were high, and Union forces crossed the Potomac and invaded Alexandria. A close friend and confidant of Abraham Lincoln, commander of the Eleventh New York Fire Zouaves Colonel Elmer E. Ellsworth, removed a secessionist flag from the roof of the Marshall House. As he made his way down the stairs, the proprietor, James W. Jackson, shot Ellsworth point-blank in the chest and killed him. Immediately after, Corporal Francis Brownell shot Jackson and bayoneted him. Brownell would get a medal of honor for his heroic actions.

Those who died at the Marshall House each came from one side of the Civil War. Each man became a martyr for the cause, and "Remember Ellsworth" and "Remember Jackson" were used as slogans and battle cries throughout the rest of the Civil War by both Union and Confederate in honor of their respective comrades.

Even though the Marshall House is long gone, the reported haunting of the Alexandrian seems to be centered on Jackson, who may be trying to protect his property even to this day. Ellsworth has been seen in the mirrors, as well as on the rooftop where he removed the rebel flag. Others have reported seeing his shadow on the stairs where he died. Jackson has been seen in that same stairwell, which makes sense since, that is where he made the life-altering decision that resulted in his death. Gunshots have also been heard in the hallways, as if the original skirmish is replaying in real time.

The sixth floor is reported to be the most haunted; it is said to be where Ellsworth's spirit takes refuge. One story in particular surrounds a couple that was staying in the hotel. They were taking the elevator, and for no reason, it stopped on the fourth floor. As the doors opened, the couple claimed, they saw a ghostly light appear on the opposite wall and disappear. No other guests got on the elevator. The hotel seemed to embrace its ghostly legend at one point, offering sixth-floor rooms to paranormal enthusiasts.

CARLYLE HOUSE

The Carlyle House was built in 1753 by John Carlyle, and the lot behind it was once home to Green's Mansion House. Carlyle was a Scottish merchant who started construction of the house in 1751 and used indentured and slave labor to build the house. Carlyle purchased two lots for the house in 1749, and he chose the location because it had easy access to trade routes, which he needed to better connect with customers. These lots were also the most expensive out of all the options. When he completed construction in 1753, his wife, Sarah Fairfax Carlyle, moved in, and on that same night, their son was born. The house was the pinnacle of the finest Georgian architecture, and it became a popular spot for social events.

But Carlyle didn't have much time to enjoy his home, as the French and Indian War was underway. General Edward Braddock took over Carlyle's home for three weeks to use as his own living quarters while he was commander-in-chief of His Majesty's forces in North America. According

Carlyle House. *Author's collection.*

to Carlyle, Braddock was not a great house guest, as he enjoyed drinking and hosting women.

The Carlyle family did have its share of tragedy. Sarah would give birth to seven children, but five of them died young. The fifth child was first to make it past childhood. Carlyle owned slaves, and ledgers and records discuss the deaths of a few slaves, including one who was lost to drowning.

Sadly, after giving birth to their seventh child, Sarah died in 1761. Just nine months later, Carlyle remarried to a woman named Sybil West. Sybil would give birth to four children, but only one survived. It seemed that Carlyle was cursed, in a way, when it came to having multiple children. Sybil's time in this world was also short-lived, as she died in 1769. Carlyle didn't remarry and died in 1780. He left the house to his fourteen-year-old son, George. George died a year later in battle, and the house remained in the family until 1827. During this time, the land that the house sat on was sold piece by piece by heirs.

After the final Carlyle family member passed, the house was purchased by furniture manufacturer James Green in 1847. He had wanted to buy the entire one-acre lot but could only get a partial amount.

When James Green owned the house, it became known as the Mansion House. Green converted another building on the property from a bank to a hotel. It was known as the Mansion House Hotel and, later, the Green Hotel. The hotel was expanded to the point where people could no longer see the Carlyle/Mansion House.

Of course, when the Civil War began, everything changed. In 1861, Green and his family had to leave the Green Hotel and the Mansion House. The hotel was converted into a military hospital, and the Mansion House became the place where the doctors and officers would live.

During World War I, the mansion became a museum. By the mid-twentieth century, the mansion and the hotel were in bad shape. NOVA Parks purchased the two buildings in 1970 and restored the Carlyle House, while the hotel was ultimately torn down.

The Carlyle House experienced its share of tragedy, between deaths of children, mothers and enslaved people and war literally coming to its front door.

In Michael Lee Pope's book *Ghosts of Alexandria*, he explains that there aren't any ghosts inside the Carlyle House; they all reside in the yard. Most of the spirits are those of children, but even Sybil has been seen outside. However, spirits have also been spotted inside the Carlyle House, including that of Sybil. The story around Sybil could be unfair because she was the second wife and there was a stigma about being the second wife and "evil stepmother"—which continues to this day. According to legend, Sybil was extremely jealous of Carlyle's first wife, Sarah. According to one story, Sybil burned all of Sarah's possessions when she moved in. Cold drafts, orbs and cold spots are blamed on Sybil.

According to the website Alexandria Ghosts, there's even a Bloody Mary–type legend around Sybil. Girls who share Sarah's name are dared to ring the doorbell and say, "Sarah, come outside!" Apparently, Sybil will answer the call instead by screaming in anger from the garden behind the house.

Pope also reports that three people fell to their deaths from the hotel's windows and their spirits also remain. Tour guides have felt tugging on their clothes in the yard and seen ghostly apparitions outside.

One of the people who fell out the window was a Union soldier who was at the hotel back when it was a Civil War hospital. He was either mentally unstable, hallucinating from pain or experiencing a side effect of pain medication when he tried to escape the hotel through one of the windows. He got caught on an overhang before falling onto the railing below. His injuries were so severe that he died just a few hours later.

Another ghost is believed to be that of a man who died in 1905 after falling while attempting to cross an overpass that connected the house and the hotel. The man's body lay in the courtyard for about twelve hours before he was examined and it was discovered that he was dead. Onlookers assumed he was drunk and had passed out.

Finally, the last poor soul who fell out of one of the windows was a tour guide named Patrick Buckley. He arrived in Alexandria and started working as a tour guide in 1910. In 1912, he was on the premises drunk when he stepped out of one of the hotel windows onto the fire escape. He then fell to his death. There were theories that Buckley had been murdered, but the autopsy report and the coroner declared his death an accident.

While the mansion was being restored, a mummified cat was discovered sealed in the foundation. This was actually a typical practice during the time, as they were seen as "good luck cats" and used to ward off evil spirits.

Did this charm actually work? If we assume that the spirits residing at the Carlyle House and the site of the old Mansion Hotel aren't evil, then it seems like it was a success.

THE RAMSAY HOUSE

The Ramsay House was once the family home of William Ramsay, one of the founders of Alexandria. He was a Scottish merchant as well as the first mayor of Alexandria, elected in 1749. The house was built around 1724, and it was purchased by the City of Alexandria in 1944 to save it from demolition. After William passed away, the house went to his son Dennis and his family and descendants. Reportedly, people in eighteenth-century period clothing are often seen in the basement.

Ramsay House. *Author's collection.*

Today, the Ramsay House serves as the Alexandria Visitor Center and is right next door to the Schafer House. It is also the starting point for Alexandria Colonial Tours, which include ghost tours.

WOODLAWN PLANTATION

Woodlawn Plantation was originally part of George Washington's Mount Vernon estate. The home was given to Washington's nephew Lawrence Lewis and his bride, Eleanor (Nelly) Parke Custis (Martha Washington's granddaughter), as a wedding present in 1799. The house had over two thousand acres of land, and it took five years to build. Woodlawn was supported by slave labor. George Washington died before Woodlawn was completed, but he often rode around the construction site to check its progress before his death. Sadly, the Lewis family often faced tragedy: out of their eight children, only three survived into adulthood.

Woodlawn was the place to be when it came to lavish parties and a thriving social scene. Anyone who was anyone was seen at social events at the massive estate. It remained in the family until Nelly and Lawrence's son sold the property in 1846. Woodlawn became a "free labor colony" where freed slaves and farmers were allowed to own portions of the land. The house went through multiple owners, but it was damaged by a hurricane and then abandoned for six years until 1896. Two brothers eventually moved into Woodlawn with their elderly mother and sixty-seven cats. These brothers had faith in the property and worked to restore it.

Woodlawn was moved from Mount Vernon over to Alexandria, and the ghosts came with the building. Today, it is a National Historic Landmark.

It seems that Woodlawn embraces its paranormal activity. Author Judy McElhaney wrote a booklet called *Ghost Stories of Woodlawn Plantation*, in which she illustrates several reports of ghosts. The paranormal activity today is related to previous residents who have called Woodlawn their home over the years. Some of the paranormal reports include seeing an apparition of George Washington himself. One of the most common sightings is Washington riding on his white horse on a moonlit night. He circles the house and then rides up and down the driveway. There's another story about a tourist who took a photo of a chair in Woodlawn and Washington's foot appeared in the picture.

It seems that long after the property was moved away from Mount Vernon, Washington keeps close watch over it to ensure it's taken care of.

THE MICHAEL SWOPE HOUSE

The Michael Swope House sits at 210 Prince Street. Today, it is privately owned, so be sure to enjoy the view from a reasonable distance. The townhouse was built around 1784–86, just a year or two after the Revolutionary War ended. It has been through multiple renovations, according to the style of its owner at the time. It was even converted into apartments at one point, but today it is a single-family home that's worth a lot of money.

Michael Swope House. *Author's collection.*

The house is named after Colonel Michael Swope, born in 1725. He was a successful soldier from York, Pennsylvania, during the Revolutionary War, and he quickly rose through the ranks. He and his family moved to Alexandria in 1784, and Swope owned a ship chandlery, meaning he provided supplies for ships and boats. The house remained in the Swope family until 1823, just three years before Swope died. Details about Swope's life are a bit muddy, though, with discrepancies between the historical marker on the house and the genealogical records.

This is where the ghost lore and the reported manifestations get interesting. In his *Big Book of Virginia Ghost Stories*, author L.B. Taylor Jr. tells the story of a poltergeist by the name of John Dixon, who was reported to be a colonial spy and erroneously executed during the Revolutionary War. Apparently, Dixon lived in the Swope home. However, there seems to be little to no evidence to support this claim, especially since the house was built after the Revolutionary War.

According to the historical marker on the house, Michael Swope was captured fairly early on in the Revolutionary War and held prisoner. He was exchanged for Benjamin Franklin's son (who was a Loyalist) after the war ended. Perhaps the stories of John Dixon and Michael Swope were merged to create a story that was pinned onto one person.

A few reports have claimed that the ghostly activity in the house dates to 1859.

Since the death of the mysterious John Dixon, people have felt a strange presence in the house. Taylor's book recounts the story of a British woman who was interested in buying the house. But as she ascended the stairs to of the master bedroom on the third floor, which is reportedly where Dixon slept, the woman stopped. She claimed that she had psychic abilities and there was a ghost present that didn't like her. This experience was attributed to Dixon's ghost and the possibility that he didn't like the woman because she was British.

CRAIK HOUSE

Dr. James Craik was a Scottish immigrant and one of the three physicians who oversaw George Washington leading up to his death. During the Revolutionary War, Craik served as a medical doctor. During and after the war, Craik became good friends, if not best friends, with Washington.

After the war, Craik opened a medical practice in Alexandria and frequently visited Mount Vernon as Washington's personal physician. Craik's house was built in 1787, and he practiced medicine from his home. When Washington fell ill, Craik was called to the house, and along with two other doctors, he treated his friend the best way he could—with bloodletting. In other words, Craik drained Washington's blood in hopes of cleansing whatever was ailing the first president. Sadly, Craik's work was in vain, as Washington passed away.

Craik House. *Author's collection.*

Since Craik passed away in 1814, his home has been well-preserved and is almost immaculate. However, there's a reason that the house is prominently featured on ghost walks in Alexandria. One of the better-known stories is about a young couple who were renting the house. On a dark and stormy night, they heard a knock at the door. When they answered it, there was a sailor in an overcoat who asked, "Where's James?" The wife, thinking her husband had a visitor, brought the sailor inside to her husband. When the sailor saw the husband, he exclaimed, "You're not James!" Instead of leaving, the sailor headed up to the second floor.

The couple then heard the sailor speak, and then someone answered him! Knowing they were home alone, the couple became incredibly concerned. Then the couple heard fighting. Terrified, they called the police. When the officer arrived, the noise upstairs ceased. The wife said, "I think they killed each other." So the officer grabbed his gun and headed upstairs, only to see nothing.

The couple ended up staying in a hotel that night, and then they moved out.

CHAPTER 2
ARLINGTON, VIRGINIA

Arlington, Virginia is a vibrant city that is often overshadowed by major tourist attractions. Arlington is also the most densely populated county in the United States. Tourists who visit the city often don't look beyond Arlington National Cemetery and the Pentagon. And yet it offers so much more. Arlington covers about 25.8 miles of Northern Virginia and sits just across the Potomac River from Washington, D.C. In fact, most Potomac River crossings originated in the area we know as Arlington.

Arlington's history dates to Colonial times, as it was part of the original land grant to Lord Fairfax. Before the area became Arlington, it was part of Alexandria Country and, eventually, Fairfax County and the Colony of Virginia in 1790. Arlington, neighbor to George Washington's Mount Vernon and home to Arlington National Cemetery, holds hundreds of years' worth of history. Even though the landscape has changed so much that it would be almost unrecognizable to residents from fifty years ago, its past is still rich.

Arlington County is probably one of the younger counties in the area, but the area is old. In 1789, part of Fairfax County was handed over to the federal government to form Alexandria County, which was part of Washington, D.C. The State of Virginia wouldn't get that part of Fairfax County back until 1846. But then it shrank in size due to the secession of Alexandria as an independent city in 1870, and it was later renamed Arlington County in 1920.

Ball-Sellers House circa 2023—one of the only homes still standing from the eighteenth century in Arlington. *Author's collection.*

The Arlington that people see today is not reflective of what Arlington used to be. The area was once mainly farmland and very rural. The only area with some sort of semblance of what Arlington is today as a city is the neighborhood of Rosslyn. The community was not very densely populated; therefore, there weren't a lot of ghost stories publicly known in the area. Arlington is also a city of transition; many people move to Arlington only to live there temporarily due to work, a military assignment or a political election, and then they leave to either return to their hometowns or settle down someplace else—taking their stories with them.

But despite people leaving, stories have remained, and ghostly happenings continue with a new set of witnesses.

ROSSLYN FIRE

On September 26, 1925, the neighborhood of Rosslyn was hit by a devastating fire. It began when six gasoline tanks belonging to the Crown Oil & Wax Company, each about two thousand gallons, caught fire. As each tank exploded, the *Washington Post* reported, "sheets of blazing gasoline" were sent in multiple directions, spreading the devastation of the fire. The fire blazed for about two hours without intervention due to a shortage in the water supply. Firefighters from the surrounding areas had to drag their hoses about two thousand feet to reach the fire.

In what could have been scenes from an action movie, two firefighters by the name of W.R. Biggs and A.B. Allison from Ballston had to leap to safety from the water tank. As each gasoline tank exploded, the firefighters had to hide behind other tanks.

Near the entrance of Fort Corcoran, which was located in the Rosslyn neighborhood. *Library of Congress.*

There was a crowd of about ten thousand people watching from a distance. But even so, there were still people too close to the fire, to the point that firefighters threatened to turn the hose on the crowd if they didn't move. The blaze of the fire could also be seen from across the river in Washington, D.C.

A few onlookers, including a group of boys, managed to save a few gasoline tanks by pushing them out of the way. After these tanks were moved, two other tanks exploded, sending burning gasoline within just a few feet of the boys. The fire resulted in about $100,000 worth of damage.

Today, the area is bustling with office buildings and professionals wandering up and down the sidewalks, unaware that the area they're moving through was once ablaze. Echoes of old-fashioned sirens, screams of men trying to get water and a town coming together to do as much as it can are lost in the city sounds of modern times. After I put out a call for stories on social media, a few people in the area reached out to me, and they were oddly specific about the activity I noted—hearing old-fashioned sirens and the screams of men—as well as feeling intense moments of heat, like there was an invisible campfire had ignited in front of them.

DEAD MAN'S HOLLOW

Today, Arlington is considered a nice area and fairly safe to live in compared to Washington, D.C., across the river. But this wasn't always the case. In the late nineteenth century, around the 1870s through the 1890s, if you were traveling on Lee Highway near Rosslyn, then you were passing through one of the most dangerous areas of the nineteenth century: Dead Man's Hollow. Back when Arlington was still part of Alexandria County, the Alexandria courthouse hosted the trials of multiple thieves and murderers.

Farmers often found themselves traveling on Lee Highway after selling their goods in D.C. Armed robbers were known to strip them of their wares and cash. It got so bad that armed guards were stationed around Dead Man's Hollow to protect the innocent. The area became notorious. It wasn't uncommon to see it mentioned in the newspaper. Murders, suicides and other heinous crimes—just another day in Dead Man's Hollow.

The tragedies of Dead Man's Hollow started around 1891, after a man by the name of Cunningham was found dead with his throat cut from ear to ear. Cunningham's death seemed to be the starting point of what would become a string of crime and murders in the area.

Crandal Mackey standing in front of Charles Knoxville's Sunday Bar, from his 1903 campaign for commonwealth's attorney. *Center for Local History, Arlington Public Library.*

With so much violence, it is no surprise that perhaps the trauma felt by the victims remains in the area today. The Rosslyn neighborhood is likely grateful that the name Dead Man's Hollow didn't stick. Today, Rosslyn is home to modern construction and regular traffic. The streets are clean and relatively safe. The shadows of the past are simply that.

Rosslyn was once an area to go if you wanted to "live in sin" and have a good time. It was not the pinnacle of a wholesome community that the city of Arlington was striving for. In an effort to "clean up the town," raids became a common occurrence in the early 1900s.

On May 30, 1904, Virginia commonwealth's attorney Crandal Mackey led raids on saloons, bordellos and gambling dens in Rosslyn and Jackson City. At the turn of the century, Rosslyn and the adjacent Jackson City had more than 38 saloons, 14 bordellos and an untold number of gambling dens and everything was always open: 7 days a week, 24 hours a day, 365 days a year.

In 1903, Crandal Mackey was elected commonwealth's attorney to put an end to the lawlessness along the Virginia side of the Potomac. He armed a party of twelve men with axes and sawed-off shotguns. They rode the train down to Jackson City, which is where the Fourteenth Street Bridge is today, and smashed it all up. Then they walked to Rosslyn and smashed up the bordellos there too, throwing whiskey into the street, setting some places on fire and destroying the gambling dens. The next day, the *Washington Evening Star* ran a two-inch headline: "Mackey Makes It Safe for Humanity in Alexandria County by Cleaning Up Rosslyn Bums."

Even though Mackey did his best to clean up the area, it seems that the trauma and those who suffered during that time still remain. The shadows of the past have been spotted by people going into modern office buildings. The screams of someone pleading for help continue to echo on the street. Several of the businesses that sit where Dead Man's Hollow stood have reported objects moving by themselves; the rush of wind, as if someone was running past them; and feelings of intense nervousness that seem to come out of nowhere.

People from the heyday of Dead Man's Hollow likely felt intense levels of anxiety due to fear of being robbed and possibly losing their life in the process; perhaps this energy continues to remain. Either way, no amount of town cleanups or bulldozers can erase the shadows of the past, and they will continue to cry out as their stories are told.

Febrey–Kincheloe House

What is now the Overlee Community used to be home to the historic Febrey-Kincheloe House. This historic mansion was built in the 1890s by wealthy steamfitter Ernest Febrey after he married his wife, Grace, in 1889. He likely had hopes and dreams for the house, as it would be the place where he would raise his children. The couple's first child, Ernest, named after his father, died in 1893 at less than a year old. A few years later, the couple welcomed a daughter named Margaret. Her childhood would be spent in the mansion her father built.

Margaret was named after her grandmother, Ernest's mother. Sadly, Margaret died at the age of fourteen on January 15, 1913, from a tubercular infection in the spine called Pott's disease. Margaret was the second child Ernest and Grace lost. It seemed that her death was too much for the couple, as they divorced not long after. Grace and her children are buried together in Oakwood Cemetery in Falls Church. Ernest married two more times after divorcing Grace. He was briefly married to Myrtle Elizabeth Bogen Febrey before she passed away at the young age of thirty-seven. Then he married Elsie Margaret Moore Febrey in 1933, and the couple remained together

Top: Febrey-Kincheloe House. *Center for Local History, Arlington Public Library.*

Bottom: Margaret Febrey's grave. *Author's collection.*

until Ernest's death. Ernest and Myrtle are buried together in Cedar Hill Cemetery in Prince George's County, Maryland.

At some point before Ernest's death in 1946, he sold the mansion to a Dr. Kincheloe. After the doctor passed suddenly, his wife established the Crestwood Sanitarium in the house in 1947. Crestwood became a rest home for Washington dignitaries.

In 1957, the people in the neighborhood around the Febrey-Kincheloe House established the Overlee Community Association. The mansion was turned into a swimming pool clubhouse as well as the residence of the manager who oversaw the community. This continued for over fifty years. It was during this time that the ghost stories began to emerge.

The manager living at the Febrey-Kincheloe House reported seeing the transparent figure of a girl wearing a Victorian dress. It is strongly speculated

Overlee Park circa 2023. *Author's collection.*

that the apparition is that of Margaret Febrey herself. They also reported hearing music downstairs, as well as phantom voices speaking and laughing in the darkness. Whenever the sounds were investigated, they immediately ceased. Margaret's apparition was also seen walking around the pool area and talking to children. She was also seen talking to guests at the clubhouse, her former home.

As the mansion continued to deteriorate, its upkeep became too great a financial burden. In 2012, the Febrey-Kincheloe House was demolished. As construction workers began the process of tearing down the historic home, once again, a young girl in a Victorian dress was seen. The girl was walking through the construction zone through the rubble. Rocks were thrown at the construction equipment, and feet were heard running through the breezeways. One construction worker even requested a transfer after seeing the apparition and refused to return to the site. There are also reports that Margaret spoke to the construction workers who were razing her home.

On the anniversary of Margaret's death, construction stopped for the day out of respect for the girl. When the Febrey-Kincheloe House was completely demolished, the board of directors of the Overlee Community Association left flowers and a note that said, "Dear Margaret, we are building you a new house. Please come visit any time." But alas, Margaret's apparition was never seen again.

WAKEFIELD HIGH SCHOOL

Wakefield High School was built in 1952 and opened for the 1952–53 school year. Because the school opened when segregation was legal in Virginia, it was an all-White school. In the early 1960s, the all-Black school, Hoffman-Boston High School, was closed, and those students moved over to Wakefield.

One of the original brick buildings held the school's theater, and it's from there that the ghostly tale emerged. It is reported that students used to sit in the balcony to listen to the piano playing by itself and watch the lights go on and off when no one was there. If you looked carefully enough, you could see the apparition of a crew member standing on the catwalk.

Rumor has it that a crew member fell from the catwalk in the 1960s, and it is this person who haunts Wakefield High School. During a chat, a longtime Arlington local who attended Wakefield mentioned that a fellow student had taken his own life, and it was believed that he haunted the theater. She also mentioned that sometimes the piano (which was on wheels) would roll around the stage, moving by itself.

In 2007, the school started making plans for modernizing local Arlington schools, and Wakefield, being one of three high schools in the area, was on the list. The original brick building that held the theater was demolished in 2013 for the sake of progress. So far, there have been no additional reports of any ghostly activity at Wakefield High School.

Wakefield High School circa 1998. *Center for Local History, Arlington Public Library.*

Arlington National Cemetery

Arlington National Cemetery is a landmark in the United States, and it is one of two national cemeteries that is maintained by the U.S. Army. Across its 639 acres, it is home to over 400,000 bodies and the famous Tomb of the Unknown Soldier. The tomb was established in November 1921 for an unidentified American service member who died during World War I. Unidentified soldiers from later wars were buried there in 1958 and 1984. Today, it stands as a reminder that not every soldier who lost their life has a name attached to their headstone.

But before the land was Arlington National Cemetery, it was the property of Confederate general Robert E. Lee. The way in which the government obtained the land is quite interesting and may have contributed to the hauntings on the property. During the Civil War, land was being acquired for military purposes, and Arlington was no exception. In 1861, Fort Ramsey was established on part of the land; it was later renamed to Fort Cass. In 1862, Fort Whipple was built nearby.

Additionally, cemeteries were filling fast all over the East Coast. By 1863, the United States Soldiers' Cemetery and Alexandria Cemetery were nearly full due to the overwhelming casualties of the Civil War. This prompted the federal government to start scoping out land for additional cemeteries—or more specifically, national cemeteries for the military. Agents went to look for suitable land and found that Lee's property, Arlington Estate, was the most suitable. It was high and free from the impact of floods. Plus, it had a beautiful view of Washington, D.C., and the land was described as "aesthetically pleasing."

Since Lee was a rebel general, denying him the use of his home made sense politically. The government officially purchased Arlington Estate in 1864 for $26,900. Lee's wife had sent an agent in attempt to pay the $92.07 in property taxes, which would have enabled her to keep the property, but the agent was turned away. The first military burial was for William Henry Christmas on May 13, 1864. The land was used not only for burial but also to house freed slaves, as well as for other military purposes.

By the end of the Civil War, the military land in Arlington, Fort Cass, had been abandoned. Fort Whipple suffered a similar fate, but the grounds were converted into the Signal School of Instruction for Army and Navy Officers in 1869, led by Brigadier General Albert J. Myer. Fort Whipple was renamed Fort Myer in 1881 after Myer passed in 1880.

Left: Arlington House. *Library of Congress, Prints & Photographs Division, HABS No. VA-443-7, reproduction number HABS VA,7-ARL,1-.*

Below: Fort Myer officers' quarters. *Library of Congress.*

Left: Tending to the injured after the crash of the Wright Military Flyer at Fort Myer circa 1908. *Library of Congress.*

Below: Fire at Fort Myer. *Library of Congress.*

Lee's grandson Custis Lee sued the U.S. government for ownership, claiming that the United States had confiscated the land without due process. Custis won the case in 1882. He sold the land back to Congress in 1882 for what would be valued at over $3 million today. Today, Arlington National Cemetery is enjoyed by millions each year. Out of those millions of people, it seems that there are ghostly voices present who still have a story to tell on the property.

OLD POST CHAPEL

Not only did the land where Arlington National Cemetery sits see considerable events during the Civil War, but it was also the site of the first aviation fatality during Orville Wright's first exhibition flights. It was also the location of the Three Sisters radio towers, the first to broadcast a voice across the United States and, eventually, the rest of the world.

The Old Post Chapel is the only chapel on the grounds of what was once as Fort Whipple. It was commissioned in 1933 by Major George Patton Jr., who wanted the chapel to also be used as a mortuary building. Ground broke in February 1934, and the chapel opened in 1935 with a dedication on April 21.

Today, the Old Post Chapel is used for weddings, for funerals for interred residents of Arlington National Cemetery who are being buried with honors and as a place of worship. Given all the history of the land

Old Post Chapel and New Gate at the Arlington National Cemetery. *Center for Local History, Arlington Public Library.*

and spiritual activities taking place, it is no surprise that there are reports of paranormal activity.

Service members have reported hearing disembodied voices in the chapel. Locked doors have unlocked by themselves. K9 units will bark at the door and refuse to go inside, especially at night. There was also a report of a woman in white being seen in the chapel, grief-stricken and still awaiting her lost love. It is believed that she threw herself from the bell tower, cursing her to haunt the grounds for the remainder of her afterlife.

Robert E. Lee Memorial

Although Robert E. Lee lost his land after the Civil War, there is a memorial to him at Arlington National Cemetery. The presence that oversees the area is believed to be that of his wife, Mary Custis Lee. If you dare speak ill of her husband, she will physically attack you.

Robert E. Lee left Arlington after the Civil War and moved to Lexington, Virginia, to become the president of Washington College with a salary of about $1,500 a year. He led a low-profile life with a job that didn't pay well. It seemed that he felt remorse for the lives lost during the war and didn't feel right making more money from the impact of the Civil War. It's very clear why Mary would be so aggressive in defending her husband's honor.

Bluemont Fire Station

I first discovered this story in September 2023 when I started my research in the area. According to a news article, there was once a haunted house where the fire station is on Fields Park and a section of George Mason Drive behind the school. There was also once an orchard and a small forest there. A slow train would come through twice a day. Today, sound of the train can still be heard, and one of the men from the station comes out and stops traffic on Wilson in ghostly form. The article briefly mentions a haunted house but gives no further details. But the fact that this story made it into a news article indicates that the occurrences were frequent enough to note in a public forum.

ARLINGTON HALL

The story of Arlington Hall is both complex and mysterious, and that's before ghosts are even mentioned. The building first opened in 1927 as the Arlington Hall Junior College for Women. This was the place to be if one wanted to climb the Arlington social ladder. The one-hundred-acre property featured a riding club, and the hall played host to social events including formal dances, balls and dinners. Yet it seems the site of Arlington Hall may have had significance during the Civil War. During an excavation of the building in 2008, an unexploded rifle shell was found under the building.

On the brink of World War II, in 1942, Arlington Hall quietly switched from a place of education for women to the headquarters of the Signal Intelligence Service. This department was dedicated to breaking Russian and German codes. But even the quiet transition and the secrecy of the department weren't enough to keep the KGB from infiltrating Arlington Hall toward the end of World War II.

The Signal Intelligence Service eventually expanded and moved its headquarters elsewhere. Arlington Hall served as a research center before becoming an office of the State Department in 1989, then the George Schultz Foreign Service Institute in 1993. During transition, weird stuff started to happen, and the ghost stories began unfolding. Employees reported hearing

Arlington Hall Girls' School students off to the nation's capital. *Library of Congress.*

moaning and groaning, and soon enough, ghosts were a hot topic among staff. Women have reported finding the stalls in the fifth-floor restroom locked from the inside, although the space under the door is too small for a person to crawl under.

As the building has seen so much activity from the living throughout its existence, it's no surprise that ghosts of the past may still be conducting business as usual. Military police standing watch in the building overnight have reported seeing a woman in a floral dress on the second floor, walking in and out of the powder room, as if she is attending a party. Just as she stops to check her makeup in the mirror, she turns and vanishes. Employees and visitors over the years have named this apparition Mary the Ghost. If you are on the ground floor of Arlington Hall in the quiet hours of the night, it is said that you will hear footsteps above you walking on the hardwood floor and then onto the carpet. Many have attributed these footsteps to the woman in the floral dress.

According to a story told by Jim Bernhardt, who was the director of foreign intelligence language curriculum development at the Foreign Service Institute, there really was a student named Mary who found out she was pregnant and committed suicide. Her father was a stable hand for the school. Before she took her life, she was seen wearing a floral dress.

After the Foreign Service Institute moved in and ghosts became a welcome topic, one employee sent invitations for a Halloween party stating, "The ghost of Mary invites you to…" One guest dressed up as a schoolmarm—a joking reference to the history of the building. The morning after the party, FSI staff unlocked the building to find the glass front of the bookshelf shattered into tiny pieces. Bernhardt said that he believed Mary was upset that they treated her memory as a joke, and now they are more respectful.

Given Arlington Hall's history of being a social hub that hosted parties, perhaps there are still spirits who are eager to continue the festivities even into the afterlife, as long as they're respectful.

Bernhardt also mentioned that a teacher of Southwest Asian languages at the FSI died suddenly. After her death, inanimate objects in her office moved by themselves, and staff members heard noises coming from her office. It seems that there is indeed a young lady who continues to wander the house long after her time there ended, and she demands respect.

The Ghost of Jim Morrison

Reported hauntings around Arlington usually consist of ghosts from the early history from the Revolutionary War, the Civil War and other major events in the area's timeline. This is rather a unique haunting because not only does it *not* involve a ghost from a pivotal moment in history, but it is also just subtle enough to be (almost) forgotten. The ghost in question was a rather notable figure in life who changed the trajectory of rock music.

That ghost is Jim Morrison.

Morrison was the lead vocalist of the infamous rock band The Doors. But before he was a rock star, he was a military kid who was forced to move around the country thanks to his father's career as a rear admiral in the United States Navy. Morrison spent parts of his childhood in San Diego. Then he completed third grade in Fairfax County, not too far from Arlington. He also spent time in Texas and New Mexico before making his way back to San Diego in middle school. Morrison attended freshman and sophomore year of high school in Alameda, California, before spending his junior and senior years at George Washington High School in Alexandria and graduating from there.

It seems that Morrison must have felt a special connection to his multiple residences in Northern Virginia. He lived in at least two addresses in Arlington and even one in Falls Church. According to an article in the *Washington Post*, one resident of a house he lived in on North Twenty-Eighth Street in Arlington has reportedly experienced Morrison's ghost, long after his passing in 1971 in Paris, France. According to the resident, Rhonda Baron, Morrison's ghost had laid down next to her on three occasions as of 2011. The ghostly rock star reportedly left a dent on the mattress. According to journalist Charlie Clark for the *Falls Church News-Press*, Baron slept in Morrison's former bedroom. Perhaps this Arlington home was where he truly felt at home and he could find rest, while saying hello to whoever entered the home.

UFO Sightings

While unidentified flying objects are not necessarily associated with ghosts, Arlington has been at the center of several UFO sightings. Since Arlington is also home to the Pentagon and across the river from Washington, D.C., perhaps it's not such a wild idea, especially when one considers that UFO sightings often coincide with major landmarks. From July 12 to 29, 1952, the D.C. area became overwhelmed with UFO sightings.

On the evening of July 19, 1952, an air traffic controller by the name of Edward Nugent at Washington National Airport in Arlington (today's Ronald Reagan National Airport/DCA) spotted several UFOs in the sky, positioned southwest of the District of Columbia. Nugent asked his colleagues to double check his equipment, and they confirmed that everything was working properly. The rest of the air traffic controllers on duty watched as the group of UFOs hovered over the White House as well as the Capitol building.

Fighter jets from New Castle Air Force Base in Delaware were sent to the area to check it out. But the UFOs disappeared. After the fighter jets left to refuel, the UFOs appeared once again. Observing this, the air traffic controllers began to believe that the UFOs had a way to intercept radio communications. By the time dawn came around, the flying objects had disappeared.

UFO sightings continue in the Arlington area and well into Northern Virginia to this day. Perhaps entities from another world have a vested interest in the area and the happenings around it.

Minor's Hill

Before the area was colonized, Minor's Hill was a popular and well-known spot for Native Americans. An important trail linked Little Falls of the Potomac River to what is now the center of Falls Church. The trail wound around the eastern and northern side of Minor's Hill.

Why the name Minor's Hill? George Minor, born in 1753, was a colonel in the Fairfax County Militia during the Revolutionary War. He led a Virginia militia detachment to fight at Bladensburg, but when they encountered escaping U.S. troops, they realized the battle was over.

In 1784, Minor became a justice of Fairfax County and in 1798 a trustee of an area called South Haven, now modern-day Rosslyn. In 1779, he was awarded quite a bit of land. He gave some of the land to Fairfax Chapel, which became the first Methodist Episcopal church in the area. Part of the land he was awarded included what is known today as Minor's Hill. In 1788, Minor obtained more land, some of which would become Arlington County.

Minor's Hill evolved from a cabin in 1814 to an expansive residence in the nineteenth and twentieth centuries. The house was named after George, and eventually the area became known as Minor's Hill, which was just over the border from Arlington into McLean. As Washington was burning during the War of 1812, First Lady Dolley Madison and her group stayed at Minor's Hill from August 26 to 27, 1814. Minor's Hill was also used strategically as an area for surveillance by both the Union and the Confederacy during the Civil War.

The house would be occupied by Minor's descendants into the second half of the twentieth century. In his book *Hidden History of Arlington County*, author Charlie Clark recounts the experience of Marion Hardy LaRow. She grew up in the historic home on Minor's Hill in the 1970s. LaRow's family spoke of a ghost who they believed was Mary Minor. During World War II, LaRow's grandmother had purchased new glassware and silverware. One day, when she was home alone, she laid them out in the old kitchen. She walked away for a moment and came back to the kitchen to find the new glassware and silverware stacked at the end of the table and the old glassware put back out.

Sadly, the historic home on Minor's Hill was torn down for development.

VIRGINIA HARDWARE COMPANY

Today, the restaurant Wilson Hardware is located on the former site of the Virginia Hardware Company. The hardware store was originally located in Rosslyn, until the business moved. According to locals, when the site was still a hardware store, it was home to a ghost or two. Some of the most common activity included the sounds of footsteps when the store was empty, usually occurring during closing time or in the early morning before opening. Merchandise moved and swung on its hooks, as if an invisible entity was checking out the products for purchase.

Top: Virginia Hardware Company circa 1930. *Center for Local History, Arlington Public Library.*

Bottom: Wilson Hardware circa 2023. *Author's collection.*

Part II

Northern Part of the Commonwealth

CHAPTER 3

MANASSAS, VIRGINIA

Today, Manassas is a bustling suburb with homes, restaurants, schools, parks and other venues for recreational activities. Located about thirty miles west-southwest of Washington, D.C., Manassas is an attractive area for people to live with its proximity to Dulles airport and the nation's capital—just a metro ride or toll road away.

But before Manassas was the town we know today, it was known as Tudor Hall, named after a prominent house in the area. During the Civil War, the area became known as Manassas Junction after the railroad junction known as Manassas Gap for the Orange and Alexandria Railroads. Throughout its early history, there were just a few houses and railroad depots, which is why the area was an attractive place for a battlefield: it had plenty of farmland and was a safe distance from densely populated areas.

The area was absolutely ravaged after the Civil War, with civilians in houses scattered around what became a battlefield. Manassas became famous around the world. After the Civil War was over, northerners started moving down to the area since land was cheaper. Both Union and Confederate veterans would eventually work together. Education also became a priority, and the Manassas Village Colored School was established in 1870 by the African American community. It would be renamed the Brown School about a year later.

The town of Manassas was officially born on April 2, 1873. At the time, the town had a population of about three hundred. The area outside and around Manassas had a population of about one thousand. The townspeople of Manassas needed support with getting roads paved; protection from fires;

creating sidewalks, saloons, livestock management; and more. The area needed support from the government and needed to establish some sort of infrastructure to support its growth.

In 1893, Jennie Dean established the Manassas Industrial School for Colored Youth, which became nationally known. The Prince William County Courthouse moved to Manassas in 1894, sparking rapid growth in the area. A 1917 ordinance enforced segregation in the area. After World War II, businesses and housing developments were on the rise, covering much of the farmland that once dominated the area. The Manassas battlefield was saved, thanks to an odd arrangement for a statue of Stonewall Jackson that's almost cartoonish. But that was the cost of historical preservation.

MANASSAS BATTLEFIELD

Although the shots at Fort Sumter in Charleston, South Carolina, marked the beginning of the Civil War, its first major battle was the First Battle of Bull Run, which happened north of Manassas on July 21, 1861. The battle was named after the Bull Run stream, which ran through the battlefield. The battle was a victory for the Confederates. In total, there were 4,878 casualties, 2,896 Union men and 1,982 Confederates. This battle also brought the realization that the Civil War would not be over and done in under ninety days, as President Abraham Lincoln had hoped.

A little over a year later, August 28–30, 1862, marked another battle that would be known as Second Manassas, also known as the Second Battle of Bull Run—again, a victory for the Confederates. The Union was absolutely crushed, and it looked likely that the Confederacy would win the war. The Union suffered a casualty rate of over fourteen thousand troops, while the Confederates lost a little over seven thousand.

With two such devastating events happening—not only with a significant number of casualties but also just over a year apart—it wouldn't be out of turn to wonder what remains in the area supernaturally. So many soldiers lost their lives, and only a few are acknowledged with markers. There are countless reports of people experiencing some kind of paranormal activity at the Manassas Battlefield. People who live near the battlefield and students who attend the nearby community college have reported having experiences for decades. Apparitions of soldiers walking the battlefield and mysterious sounds of cannon fire are common occurrences around the battlefield.

BULL RUN STONE BRIDGE

The Bull Rune Stone Bridge was built in 1815, which means it stood witness to both Battles of Bull Run. People have reported seeing shadows of Civil War soldiers as well as the faint sound of cannon fire on the bridge.

THE DEEP CUT

An area known as the Cut or the Deep Cut was named after the railroad cut that was present during the Second Battle of Manassas and remains today. It was the center of an extremely bloody battle between Union and Confederate soldiers on August 30, 1862. The Confederates took up a defensive position on the elevated railroad bed.

Tee Morris and Phil Rossi of Old Spirits Investigations (OSI) paid a visit to the Cut, and they reported having interesting experiences. When they came to a little spot off to the side of the battlefield near the cut, they saw animal bones everywhere. They didn't know what the animals were, but nonetheless, they were a bit shaken up and felt unsettled.

Morris and Rossi got out their equipment, including a REM-Pod and a MEL meter, and attempted to establish communication. They believe they talked with an entity that appeared to be a soldier. Other equipment, like a word generator, was also running, and words popped up that made sense in the context of the conversation. Morris's wife, Pip, also had a strange experience: she reported that it felt like someone was walking behind her. As she was listening to the session on the recorder, she thought she heard laughter and a child's voice.

THE ZOUAVE SOLDIERS

Another common occurrence at the Manassas battlefield is the appearance of a Zouave soldier near the New York Monument. The Zouave regiment modeled their uniform after the French Zouaves and underwent the regiment's unique training structure. The Fifth New York Infantry Regiment was a Zouave regiment that was under the command of Colonel Governor K. Warren. They were also known as the Duryee's Zouaves, as they were sponsored by a prominent mahogany importer named Abraham Duryee.

During the Second Battle of Manassas, General Pope had the regiment in the railroad cut on the battlefield, much to the men's confusion. At four o'clock in the afternoon on August 30, the Fifth Regiment was pelted by bullets. What started as hundreds of soldiers became sixty when the regiment mustered at Henry Hill. It was an absolute slaughter. The regiment lost about three hundred soldiers in less than ten minutes.

Usually, the ghostly soldier is seen at night, under the moonlight. People have reported seeing the soldier wandering the area, as if he is looking for something. Once they get a closer look, they are horrified to see that the man has no head. One witness saw a Zouave soldier over the course of several nights. When others tried to approach the soldier, he dissolved right in front of their eyes.

Witnesses have also seen about forty or fifty Zouave soldiers over by what is known as New York Avenue through their binoculars. The problem, though, was that these soldiers' faces were white, and there were black holes where their eyes should have been.

A Civil War reenactor was camping on the battlefield when she saw a man in a Zouave uniform. He lifted his hand and proceeded to move toward her. She ran in fright. Apparently, her husband saw the same man, only this time he had a green glow about him as he floated in a figure 8 pattern.

The appearance of the Zouave soldier became so common that it was investigated by a parapsychologist named Arthur Berger. When Berger took the witnesses to investigate the spot, they seemed to have experiences once again, while Berger did not. When Berger got his photos developed, he was surprised to see that the prints were blank.

Could it be that these poor souls of the Fifth New York Regiment are still replaying the day they died? Why are they hanging around the battlefield? Could it be that they're trapped? There's also the possibility that this could be a residual haunting. There's a theory that when a great deal of trauma that takes place, the energy remains and replays itself like a broken record. That could also explain the strange feelings and sightings. Or is it possible that these soldiers are still trying to do their job and complete their unfinished business?

Stone House

During the Battle of First Manassas, a stone house stood strong as it took sprays of bullets and cannon fire. The Stone House was built in 1848 and wore many hats during its existence. It was a popular place as a tavern, inn and wagon stop for weary travelers. But the visitors weren't necessarily the best of the best of Virginia's citizens. Many were rough-and-tumble cattle ranchers and teamsters who liked to drink. In addition to being a tavern, it was once a private home.

During both Battles of Manassas, the Stone House was converted into a makeshift hospital. It could barely support all the wounded men. There were as many as thirty-two wounded soldiers in the house at one time. Soldiers died where they lay, and they weren't removed right away. There were men in the cellar wounded and covered in mud. As soldiers waited for treatment, a few carved their names into the woodwork.

Reports of hauntings at the Old Stone House date to 1866, as noted in the book *Surry of Eagle's Nest* by Confederate veteran John Esten Cooke.

Stone House during the Second Battle of Bull Run. *Library of Congress.*

Stone House circa 2023. *Author's collection.*

The author refers to the house as the Old Stone House as well as the Haunted House.

Legend also has it that the house was cursed. The curse was reportedly placed on the family who lived in it after the Civil War. A man named Henry Ayres owned the house, and when he was on his deathbed in 1902, he asked his son to put artillery shells into the wood as a means to attract tourists and make some money from those interested in the Civil War. Six more members of the Ayres family would lose their lives from various causes, that would all be blamed on the curse.

When visitors come to the Stone House, they often report a negative presence. The entity especially doesn't like it if someone has fallen asleep on the job. Former park rangers have also come forward to make their stories about the Stone House known. Now, sometimes the National Park Service isn't thrilled about paranormal stories going around about the battlefield and its historic buildings, because they tend to attract people who end up trespassing in the middle of the night. So active park rangers aren't known to admit that there's any sort of haunting, because they don't want to become part of the problem—or worse, lose their jobs.

Park ranger protocol includes locking the door of a location behind you whenever you go in or out to ensure that guests don't come in. A friend of Mark Nesbitt, a former park ranger who broke the story of the hauntings at Gettysburg, reported that he and fellow park rangers were working in the basement of the Stone House when they started hearing the sound of footsteps coming from the floor above them. Thinking that a guest had come in, they went upstairs to check out the situation. When they reached the top, there was no one else in the house, and the door was locked.

HENRY HOUSE

Casualties are inevitable during war. But soldiers aren't the only ones who lose their lives. Even though rules of engagement and war protocol try to protect citizens as much as possible, there will always be a few who meet an incredibly tragic end. The area known as Henry House Hill was the location of such a tragedy.

Just a few yards away from the Manassas Battlefield Park Visitor Center is a house that was built in 1870 and is supposed to be a replica of a house built in 1812 by Thomas King and demolished after the Civil War. There is a small family plot with a few headstones in front of the house, with a monument to the Battle of Bull Run in the back.

If you look at the headstones in the family plot, you'll see the name Judith Henry. Judith met a terrifying and violent end to her life. In 1828, Judith's husband, Henry, bought the house for his wife and their future three children, John, Ellen and Hugh. In addition to the house, Henry also bought several acres and a huge farm. However, money soon became a problem, and Henry was forced to sell. Henry's sudden death only expedited more selling of the land, as Judith was trying to survive as a single mother, now widowed, with three children. One thing she loved, though, was her house. John and Hugh would leave the farm to become well-loved schoolteachers, while Ellen stayed home to care for the elderly Judith, and they purchased a slave named Lucy to assist.

Henry House stood opposite Henry Hill. As the First Battle of Bull Run was starting, both Union and Confederate soldiers stood on a strategic spot around Henry Hill and Judith's farm—which, unfortunately, put Henry House right in the middle of the crossfire. Initially, the plan was to move Judith to a neighbor's house about a mile away. Unfortunately, the battle prevented this, so the plan changed: move Judith to the farm's springhouse. But that wasn't much safer, so Judith asked to go back home.

During the First Battle of Manassas, eighty-five-year-old Judith Henry ended up lying in her bed with shells and gun fire raging around her. The

Union didn't realize that her house, Henry House, was occupied by civilians. Judith's daughter Ellen ended up inside the chimney for additional protection. Cannon fire hit the house hard, and Judith was knocked out of bed, injuring her head and neck; she also lost her foot. The Union Military Commission was furious that an elderly woman had been caught in the crossfire. The Union reported that Confederate snipers had entered the house to get a better shot, justifying the tragic move.

Judith died later that day, becoming the first official civilian casualty of the Civil War. Ellen, miraculously, survived the battle, but all the gun and cannon fire rendered her deaf. By the time the First Battle of Manassas was over, Henry House was in shambles. On June 13, 1865, Union veterans erected a monument to the fallen Union soldiers behind Henry House.

Judith wasn't the only person to die in the house during the battle. A Union soldier who lost his life trying to shoot snipers has reportedly been seen in the hallway. Sightings of both Judith and Ellen are often reported. Not only did Judy love the house, but Ellen did as well. Given that Judith lost her life after refusing to leave her house, it makes sense that she would still be around. In photos of the house, faces have been spotted in the windows. Visitors have seen a woman on the second floor looking out and smiling at visitors.

One of the most startling stories that has come out about Henry House is the sighting of a woman in a white nightgown and bonnet walking outside, as if taking a stroll. She has been seen more than a few times walking along the path around Henry House. The identity of the woman is unknown, but witnesses theorize that it's either Judith or Ellen.

CANNON BRANCH FORT

Cannon Branch Fort is an old Civil War fort that is believed to have been used by Union forces between 1863 and 1864, mainly to defend the surrounding railroad lines.

For a long time, this has been the favorite spot of OSI investigator Phil Rossi. Because it is such a unique location and he didn't want it to be tainted by oversaturation of investigators, he kept the spot to himself until recently. Today, the area is a city park that is open to the public from sunrise to sunset.

According to Rossi, the area has a particular energy, and the location almost has a character and personality of its own. Nestled behind an

Cannon Branch Fort site circa 2023. *Author's collection.*

industrial park, there is a pond where people can fish; visitors can also run and take walks, among other activities.

But the area is more than just the former site of a Civil War fort. Indigenous cultures occupied the area before being driven out.

It seems that the area has energies similar to those of a large-scale Civil War battlefield. Rossi and his investigation partner, Tee Morris, have had activity on their REM-Pod there. Whoever or whatever is haunting the area seems to have an affinity for music and is very responsive. Ghost-hunting gadgets light up. Rossi's wife, Tina, felt like she was being touched. They also heard was sounded like a voice calling out Rossi's name.

Rossi, Morris, their wives and a friend once conducted an Estes session in the area. During the session, one of the group asked the presence who was there. The presence responded: Tina (Rossi's wife), Rossi and Pip. Morris, feeling left out, asked the spirit why he wasn't named, and then the voice said, "Morris."

While Rossi, Morris and their wives plus special guests have yet to identify what is haunting the area, they have concluded that the entity is definitely intelligent. There is also residual energy remaining from the people who once occupied the area, as well as those involved in past conflicts.

Interestingly, Cannon Branch Fort has been the location of a UFO sighting. In October 2008, one person reported that they were driving on Godwin Drive heading south when they saw a strange bright light on their right over near Cannon Branch. They were in their truck alone, and it was around midnight. They had stopped at a diner for a late dinner, and they were wide awake. The anonymous person stated that they saw a large, round object with an extremely bright light coming out of it hovering in the sky. The person made sure to mention that there were no other cars nearby at this time. They pulled over to record the sighting on their phone to show their wife later. After parking, they got out of the truck, but then the object flew upward and was gone. The person noted that they felt a big draft, and the area smelled of an electrical burn. Perhaps there is something more going on besides just ghostly presences.

Candy Factory

The ARTfactory in Old Town Manassas sits in an old candy factory. Today, it is a hot spot not only for the arts but also for paranormal activity. But the hauntings surrounding the building aren't so black and white—or even simple.

One of the earliest tragedies that happened nearby occurred in 1855 when a brakeman named John Brawner tried to jump between train cars, missed the mark and was cut in half as a result.

The area itself is riddled with history surrounding the Civil War. During the Battles of Manassas, the area was an empty lot that was used as a Confederate camp known as Camp Pickens. There, injured and sick soldiers were treated.

After the Civil War, a man by the name of Hampton Brenton bought the land, and there he built a tavern and hotel called the Brenton Hotel. In August 1872, thirty-eight-year-old George Pearson died at the Brenton Hotel after a brief illness. In 1899, two men by the name of Thomas King and John Harris were killed in a railway accident.

In May 1900, Ohioan C.A.S. Hopkins founded the Hopkins Candy Factory and set up operations on West Street in downtown Manassas. There, he produced an assortment of candies like rock candy, stick candy, coconut bars and peanut bars, all from a sixteen-by-twenty-foot building with around twenty-five employees. Sales were made thanks to traveling salesman who traveled by wagon and train, carrying and selling the sweets wholesale to general stores around the area. However, in 1905, the Brenton Hotel was destroyed by a fire, which nearly took out Hopkins's factory. Seeing an opportunity, Hopkins bought the burnt-out lot on Battle Street. There, he built a modern factory, a four-story brick structure. Construction

The Candy Factory today, now known as the ARTfactory. *Author's collection.*

started in 1907, and the factory opened in 1908. It was considered one of the most modern factories in the area, with machinery to dip chocolates as well as create an assortment of creams, jellies and more. There were multiple salesman in almost every state east of the Mississippi selling Hopkins Candy.

But then the company mysteriously ceased operation in 1917, despite being a successful business. The company sold the building, and it passed through the hands of multiple owners, including the Manassas Feed and Milling Company.

In December 1922, tragedy struck the city of Manassas. Four young men—Taylor Weir (nineteen), John Good (seventeen), Edwin Randolph Freeman (nineteen) and George Spencer (nineteen)—were on the train tracks a few days before Christmas. There are various stories about why the young men were on the tracks. Some say it was a crossing accident while trying to catch the train, while others claimed that the boys were driving around with no particular destination in mind. Either way, the boys were in George Spencer's car, which was struck by a freight train that was backing up southward around eleven thirty at night. The car was dragged about three hundred feet. The bodies were moved to the train station so that they could be seen under the lights, and Taylor's father, Robert, a policeman, was tasked with identifying them. Imagine Robert's horror and heartbreak as a father when he recognized his own son, saying, "Oh my God, it's Taylor!" The boys' funerals were held on Christmas day.

The building was eventually sold to the Southern States Manassas Cooperative in the 1930s. In 1980, Caton and Mae Merchant converted it into a tire warehouse.

Realizing the building's historical significance, the Merchants sold the Candy Factory to the City of Manassas in 1998. The Candy Factory went through restoration starting in 2001 under the guidance of the Manassas Museum. In 2002, it was leased to the Center for the Arts of Greater Manassas, and a theater as well as a gallery and studio classrooms were built. The Candy Factory, now known as the ARTfactory, hosts classes, performances art galleries and more.

Phil Rossi and Tee Morris of OSI have investigated the location several times, and the activity there remains fairly consistent. They've heard voices in the building and captured a number of EVPs. The top floor is the theater. There, people have reported seeing shadow figures, as well as apparitions of people walking around onstage. During investigations, OSI has had some intense spirit box sessions. They've managed to identify a spirit named George and encountered many incredible sounds like walking and banging.

On the second floor, there is a women's restroom that is one of the most haunted spots in the area. Women have reported hearing voices in the bathroom, as well as knocking on one of the stall doors when the user is alone. During one investigation, while in this restroom, Rossi asked the entity for a name. His device produced the name Edwin. Overall, OSI has concluded that the former Candy Factory is a great spot for paranormal investigations.

ANNABURG

Annaburg is a historic house that was built as a summer home for Robert Portner and his family. The City of Manassas purchased the property in 2019 and started a massive effort to not only restore the house but also turn the area into a park.

Annaburg was built in 1862 by Prussian brewer Robert Portner and named after his wife, Anna. Portner mainly worked out of Alexandria and was running several breweries in the area. He made a considerable amount of money selling beer to soldiers during the Civil War. It is also believed that his house was the first of its kind to have a mechanical air-conditioning system. Since Portner was brewing beer, he needed a refrigeration system to keep his

Annaburg circa 2024. *Author's collection.*

concoctions fresh. In 1878, he created the first "refrigeration machine" for his beer business. He eventually expanded the idea to Annaburg, pouring cold water down copper pipes to battle against the heat.

After Portner passed away in 1906, his family didn't visit Annaburg as much as they used to when he was alive. Over the years, Annaburg fell into disrepair, and vandals started breaking into the house. There were periods of abandonment, especially during World War II. The original copper piping was pilfered during the war. At that time, copper was exceptionally valuable.

In 1947, the family sold the home and auctioned off the assets inside. In 1961, Annaburg became a geriatric home called Manassas Manor Nursing Home. Two additional wings were built on the sides of the manor to accommodate more patients. Eventually, though, there were too many patients, and Annaburg grew overcrowded. In response, a larger facility was built behind Annaburg, and operations at the house completely stopped. The building closed in 2005.

Eventually, the house was slated for demolition. Knowing the historical value of the home, the Manassas community came together to save it, and the city purchased it in 2018.

In December 2021, Annaburg was added to the Virginia Department of Historic Places. The house has since been painted white, but recent restoration efforts include returning Annaburg to its original color scheme from when Portner lived there.

Tee Morris and his wife, Pip, were asked by the City of Manassas to check out the house and took me to Annaburg with them. As we pulled into the parking lot, I was awestruck by just how massive the structure was, and I immediately became aware of a female energy, as if a woman was watching us through the windows. The immediate emotional vibe I got was that the woman was confused by our presence, especially since we were calling her by name.

I fired up my Phasmabox, Morris got out his equipment and we started a communication session. What transpired was rather surprising for me, as we were getting intelligent responses on the Phasmabox. Using the GhostTube SEER app, we were also treated to AI-generated imagery. Visuals of a crowded room were shown to us. When we started talking about brewing beer, our favorite beers and more, that seemed to spark some interesting responses on various pieces of equipment. Toward the end of our session, GhostTube SEER showed us a lonely old woman all by herself. Needless to say, this visual broke our hearts. Morris and Pip reassured the spirits that they would be back eventually.

As Annaburg has started the process of reopening, and the City of Manassas is already partnering with a paranormal investigation team to verify claims, there's some promise of paranormal research in the future. If you find yourself visiting Annaburg, be sure to say hello to the resident spirits and them know how much you love the house.

CHAPTER 4
LOUDOUN COUNTY

The land that Loudoun County sits on was originally inhabited by the Sioux (Manahoac), Algonquin, Iroquois and Piscataway tribes before the 1722 Treaty of Albany, which led the tribes to abandon all lands east of the Blue Ridge Mountains. In 1659, King Charles II gifted a large amount of land to seven English noblemen, including what's now Loudoun County. The area sits right along the Virginia-Maryland border and is about forty-three miles northwest of Arlington, Virginia.

LEESBURG, VIRGINIA

The town of Leesburg was established in 1758 and today serves as the seat of government for Loudoun County.

Leesburg experienced significant growth during the nineteenth century, only for it to be halted and stunted due to the Civil War, which was right in the town's backyard. Much of the ghostly activity is directly connected to the Civil War.

One of the most notable battles, the Battle of Ball's Bluff, certainly overshadows the town and is connected to several of the hauntings in the area. The trauma from that battle still permeates the town, which now serves as a major tourist attraction given its proximity to wine country.

Loudoun National Bank and King Street in downtown Leesburg. *Library of Congress.*

BALL'S BLUFF BATTLEFIELD

About two miles northeast of Leesburg is the Ball's Bluff Battlefield and National Cemetery. On October 21, 1861, the Battle of Ball's Bluff took place at this precise location. In this early battle of the American Civil War, the Union Army suffered a humiliating and devastating defeat. Major General George B. McClellan, who was commander of the Army of the Potomac at the time, was hoping to stage an attack that would make the Confederates evacuate their troops away from Leesville. The attack itself was a disaster and resulted in a tremendous number of casualties for the Union, with the Confederacy taking very little damage, if any. Many Union soldiers were pushed over the bluff by the Confederates and drowned in the Potomac River. Seeing this horror, hundreds of Union soldiers chose to surrender instead of attempting to escape over the bluff. Fifty-four soldiers are buried in the on-site cemetery.

One of the earliest accounts of paranormal activity at Ball's Bluff dates to the 1950s, when a group of teenagers visited the area. They had planned on wandering around the area, but after hearing screams from an unseen source, they decided it would be best to return to their vehicle.

Slain Union soldiers during the Battle of Ball's Bluff. *Library of Congress.*

The retreat of Union soldiers during the Battle of Ball's Bluff. *Library of Congress.*

But after starting the car, when the teenagers tried to accelerate, it simply wouldn't move. It was almost like someone was preventing the car from moving. Eventually, the teens managed to wrangle themselves free, and they zoomed to one of their homes. When the teens got out of the car, they did a full examination and found the remnants of muddy handprints on the trunk of the car.

The teens recounted the incident to their parents. The parents decided to go back out to Ball's Bluff themselves to confirm that there wasn't additional mischief or foul play at hand. When the parents arrived, the area was oddly quiet—almost too quiet. They rolled their windows down and sat in the darkness, quietly listening for anything questionable. As they sat, they couldn't help but notice that the branches of one of the trees were stretching and swaying up and down toward one of the headstones, almost like an outstretched arm trying to point them in the right direction.

Other visitors to Ball's Bluff saw Civil War soldiers scaling the side of the cliff from which Union soldiers once fell to their demise. Screams continued to be heard.

Curious about more current paranormal experiences, I talked to Phil Rossi of Old Spirits Investigations. He told me that Ball's Bluff is one of his favorite spots because you can go out there during the day with minimal equipment. He recounted to me one experience he had while visiting the grounds around seven o'clock in the morning. Rossi noted that while nothing happened, he experienced an amazing feeling of being in touch with something bigger than himself. He mentioned that time slowed down, which enriched the connection he was feeling.

During his subsequent visits, Rossi came to believe that a soldier that goes by Tom haunts the area. Tom made himself known to Rossi over the spirit box as well as during an EVP session. Rossi heard, "It's Tom" during these sessions.

When I visited Ball's Bluff to take photos of the area, I was very much taken in by the energy, which I found similar to what Rossi described. I visited Ball's Bluff about two months before I heard Rossi's story. I also took video, and on reviewing it, I heard several things. During a video of the front area of the park where the benches are, around the education area, I caught a very odd sound that resembled a muffled voice. I've yet to determine what it was I heard. In another video I filmed of the small cemetery at Ball's Bluff, you can hear the yelling of men, almost like in a fight or a battle. This was a cold January day, and I was the only one in the park besides a gentleman who was walking back to his car. Could there be residual energy left over from the battle that's replaying over and over again?

Ball's Bluff overlooking the river circa 2023. *Author's collection.*

GEORGE HEAD HOUSE

You can have a cup of coffee at the Trinity House Café and Market, which was once the home of a Tory Revolutionary War soldier by the name of George Head. It is believed that George himself is buried in the basement of the home. Windows have been reported to open by themselves; the reason for this is believed to be that George always wanted fresh air in the home, even in the bitter cold of winter.

George Head House/ Trinity House Café and Market, 2023. *Author's collection.*

PAXTON HOUSE

The Paxton House was a school at the time this book was written. It was once one of the largest houses in Leesburg, and it was a private home and before becoming an orphanage. With thirty-two rooms total, there was space to spare. Some of the most notable activity involves the presence of children, although the house is empty. The house sits on the property that is known

Paxton House circa 2020. *Rebecca Slaughter Boyer.*

as the Carlheim Estate. The infamous battle of Ball's Bluff took place on the edge of the property. It is not uncommon to see the spirits of Civil War soldiers from the aftermath of that battle.

GLENFIDDICH HOUSE

During the Civil War, the Glenfiddich House was known as Harrison Hall. It became a makeshift hospital during the Battle of Ball's Bluff. One of the soldiers brought there to be treated was Colonel Erasmus Burt of the Mississippi Regiment of the Confederate States Army. He was also a friend of the Harrison family. At first, he was placed on the floor of the front parlor room before he was taken upstairs. He did not recover from his wounds and died in the home. But it seems as though Burt never left his quarters. A mysterious bloodstain appears on the floor of the front parlor room where he lay and then disappears. Witnesses have reported seeing the impression of a body in the bed where he died. The tapping of a ring on the banister has also been heard. Burt attended West Point and had the ring to show for it.

Glenfiddich House, 2024. *Author's collection.*

LYNCH HOUSE

Just across the street from the Glenfiddich House stands another haunted house. The Lynch House is home to its own Woman in White story. In this case, she has a name: Liza Thompson. Liza was a Civil War widow. Before her husband left for the war, he gave her the deed to the house for safekeeping. During the nineteenth century, women were not allowed to own property, so giving her the deed to the house was a smart move. However, the banker who oversaw the deed had passed away. The banker's wife found the deed to Liza's house and tried to claim ownership. After a thirteen-year court battle for the house, Liza was able to keep her home. Today, there are reports of Liza's spirit appearing at the foot of beds as well as walking down the halls. Given how hard Liza had to fight for her home, it's not surprising that she isn't eager to leave.

Eliza House circa 2024. *Author's collection.*

UNION CEMETERY

Union Cemetery was established in 1855 on the outskirts of Leesburg as a public cemetery open to people of all faiths. One of the most prominent ghost stories associated with the cemetery is that of a Union soldier whose shadow has been seen roaming the grounds.

OATLANDS PLANTATION

During the time of slavery, Black people were put through regular bouts of hard labor and stripped of their humanity. Built in 1804, Oatlands was a major wool and wheat producer with over 3,500 acres and as many as eighty-four enslaved people working there. Today, the historic site is about 260 acres.

Today, the house still stands and serves as a museum. Over the years, various people—from visitors to museum staff—have reported unusual activity. Visitors have heard footsteps and voices, only to find that no one else is in the house. Doors open and shut on their own. There have even been reports of people smelling roses when they're out of season and there aren't roses in the house. One visitor at Oatlands reported hearing furniture dragging across the floor, as if someone was rearranging a room. When the visitor asked the guide about it, they were shocked to hear that nothing of the sort was going on.

Oatlands Plantation circa 2023. *Author's collection.*

Above: Oatlands Plantation circa 2023. *Author's collection.*

Right: Staircase at Oatlands. *Library of Congress.*

Leesburg Presbyterian Church

The Leesburg Presbyterian Church was built in 1804 and is home to a ghost named Lillias Haney. She was a lifetime member of the church, dedicating her life to her congregation. She never married, nor did she have children. Lillias served as the choir director. After she passed away in 1963, it became apparent that she never left her beloved church.

Sightings of Lillias have been reported throughout the years, like one in 1970 when the new choir director saw a woman wandering the pews. She has also been seen in the choir loft, where she seems to monitor the choir and music program, making sure it is top notch. It is also said that one night, on New Year's Eve, a roaring wind blew through the church, making the closet hangers rattle together. All the doors and windows were closed.

Leesburg Courthouse

Like most locations in Virginia, Leesburg has its own problematic stories connected to slavery. The haunting surrounding the Leesburg Courthouse is one such tale. As mentioned in the introduction, some have to use ghost stories as a filter before being able to face the troubled and disturbing history connected to their own town or ancestors. Back in the late '90s, ghost tours of Leesburg used to feature the story of an enslaved man named Mercer, who was convicted of murder and hanged in 1768 near the Leesburg Courthouse grounds. His body was also quartered as a message to other slaves, in order to deter an uprising. According to a 1999 article in the *Washington Post*, the haunting of the courthouse is believed to be connected to Mercer, as his spirit wanders the halls, hoping to finally find justice. Truly, it's a heartbreaking story and not spooky at all. I only mention this story to encourage you to take a moment to remember him not as a ghost story but as a human being who was stripped of his rights and humanity.

4 Loudoun Street

Home to one of the most famous ghost sightings in Leesburg is an old house that is used today as an office building. The top floor of the home was once used as an archive facility where *National Geographic* employees catalogued old

Left: Leesburg Presbyterian Church. *Author's collection.*

Below: Leesburg Municipal Grounds. *Author's collection.*

4 Loudoun Street. *Author's collection.*

photos. In his book *Haunted Alexandria and Northern Virginia*, J.J. Smith describes an event that took place in 1972. While working on photos from the Civil War, the all-female staff noticed a little girl with blonde hair wearing a white nightgown. She appeared to be about three years old. The girl poked her head through the open doorway and said, "Seek!" The employees had just returned from lunch having had a bit of wine, so they didn't say anything for fear that they would sound crazy. However, the little girl appeared once more two weeks later. She exclaimed, "Let's play hide and seek!" The employees followed her, but she completely disappeared.

Benjamin Thornton House

The Benjamin B. Thornton House, located at 17 Loudoun Street, is currently occupied by a consulting firm. But it is also home to one of Leesburg's most notorious stories. It was built around 1780–1800 as a tavern. Since then, it seems that the building has had various short-term tenants. Employees have reported seeing the ghost of a woman who says, "Peekaboo!" She also wraps her hands around their coffee cups. She's been described as around five-feet tall, thirty-five years old, long-haired and wearing an empire nightgown. A paranormal investigation team called the Virginia Scientific Research Association (VSRA) was brought in to assess

Benjamin Thornton House circa 2024. *Author's collection.*

the situation. They conducted historical research and couldn't identify the woman that the employees were seeing.

Investigators got a break in the case in 1999 when an elderly woman attending a ghost tour claimed she knew the Peekaboo Ghost, as she used to have tea and sandwiches with her. Apparently, Peekaboo's connection to Leesburg was her sister, who lived in the town. Peekaboo's cause of death was cancer. One of her last wishes before she passed in Cincinnati, Ohio, was to spend time with her sister in Leesburg. Apparently, the woman now known as the Peekaboo Ghost said that she felt at home and loved in Leesburg, which could be why her spirit has been seen there. The elderly woman couldn't recall the Peekaboo Ghost's name, but she was able to describe her in great detail, validating her story.

19 EAST MARKET STREET

The building at 19 East Market Street used to be a tavern, and taverns are often known as paranormal activity hot spots, as it is theorized that ghosts and spirits are drawn to electromagnetic fields (EMFs) for energy. According to a woman named Keeler, Virginia Scientific Research Association (VSRA) vice president, it was not uncommon for her group's paranormal investigation equipment to run out of batteries throughout the night at 19 East Market

19 East Market Street. *Author's collection.*

Street, as the EMFs would drain the batteries. Keeler also used to work in the building and reported seeing a woman on the first floor, wearing a black dress with a veil and crying. When she alerted her employees that there was a woman crying, they asked her if she was wearing a black veil.

LOUDOUN MUSEUM

The Loudoun Museum has existed in many different iterations. It started off as an African American speakeasy in 1730 before becoming an office for the first African American doctor in Leesburg. According to Olivia DeWan, writer at Leesburg's *County Chronicle*, a female spirit haunts the museum, and she was discovered about thirty years ago. A psychic medium was even brought in, who identified the spirit as a woman named Elizabeth. Reports of paranormal activity include doors flying open by themselves as well as the sound of feminine footsteps passing from one side of the building to the other. Elizabeth has been seen by employees, who sometimes see only the fabric of her plaid skirt. A second psychic was even brought in, and they were able to describe Elizabeth's outfit in a way that matched the employees' descriptions.

Above: Side view of the Loudoun Museum. *Author's collection.*

Right: Front of the Loudoun Museum. *Author's collection.*

Sterling, Virginia

Sterling is not far from Leesburg and other historically haunted towns, so a few ghosts here and there are to be expected. Located about twenty-eight miles from Washington, D.C., along the Potomac River, Sterling started off as primarily farmland with a focus on cattle, dairy and meat and a population of around two hundred. When a railroad depot was established in 1860, goods could be transported faster and in larger quantities than ever before, and business boomed. When the construction of Dulles International Airport started in 1959, Sterling's population exploded.

But Sterling is also dealing with the ongoing issue of historic locations being leveled for the sake of modernization and development. Sterling, with a population of about thirty thousand, is one of the younger towns in the area to be officially named. But the area has been long known to be home to farmland. Sitting east of Leesburg and a short drive away from Dulles, Sterling is tucked into the corners outside of the airport.

Much of the remnants of "Old Sterling" are nearly gone, including historic houses that hosted presidents such as James Buchanan.

Farmhouse and cane near Sterling. *Library of Congress.*

Cost Plus World Market

While seemingly a random place for a haunting, it seems that the Cost Plus World Market in a Sterling shopping center is haunted. Employees have reported seeing a shadow figure, hearing footsteps caused by an unseen entity and "shopping carts crashing against shelves for no reason." The activity typically occurs late at night and stirs up plenty of unsettling feelings for the employees who are clocked in.

Cascades Community

One anonymous person told their story of living in the haunted Cascades community of Sterling. They reported often hearing voices in the basement as well as footsteps all over the house. They also heard mysterious tapping on the floors and doors opening and closing by themselves. Mysterious orbs would appear around the person when they were on an online call.

Ghostly Wanderers

Every region in the United States—even around the world—has a ghost story about a road or some ghostly hitchhiker. Sterling's version is the tragic story of a girl who was kidnapped and murdered on a dirt road, today known

Sterling houses at a crossroads. *Library of Congress.*

as Maries Road. It seems that the murdered girl was named Marie, hence the road's name. Legend says that if you drive down this road late at night and honk your horn three times, Marie will appear in the tree line where her house used to be. According to the story, Marie was lured out in the same way the night she lost her life.

THE CRYING GIRL

There is another story of a young girl who ran away from home. She managed to get out, but by the time night fell, she had decided it was time to go home. Sadly, on her way home, she was hit by a drunk driver and killed. While there isn't any historical record of this incident, interestingly, people have seen the apparition of a young girl walking along the road and sobbing.

THE DARK MAN

Legend says that a man in a dark overcoat wanders the streets of Sterling at night. He is seen with a cigarette in his mouth. He doesn't react when people call out to him, acknowledge him or even display fear of him.

PURCELLVILLE, VIRGINIA

Purcellville has a population of nearly ten thousand today. It's a quiet, small town in Northern Virginia, with really only one claim to fame: it is the birthplace of Orville and Wilbur Wright's mother, Susan Koener. It's just under ten miles west of Leesburg and about twenty miles from the West Virginia border. It's about as far north as one can get in Northern Virginia, since it's less than fifteen miles from the Maryland border.

THE PURCELLVILLE LIBRARY

The Purcellville Library was established in 1937 during the height of the Great Depression and opened in 1938. The library received federal funding, as well as generous contributions from a wealthy woman by the name of

Gertrude Robey. *Loudoun County Public Library, Purcellville.*

Gertrude Robey. Gertrude, the chief librarian, was well known as a charismatic woman who ran the library with rigidity. She also alleged to be a Southern sympathizer. Given that she was born in 1883 in Culpeper Country, Virginia, and her father, the Reverend Fleet Henderson James, served as a private in the Virginia Calvary Sixth Regiment Company A, Gertrude having ties to the South and its nineteenth-century ideals isn't too surprising.

Gertrude was known to dress in all black and wear a black, wide-brimmed hat that she called her "emancipation hat." The reason Gertrude was assumed to be a Southern sympathizer was that she banned Harriet Beecher Stowe's *Uncle Tom's Cabin* from the shelves of the Purcellville Library. She also wouldn't allow romance books, especially if they had even a hint of something risqué. Given that the library was the only one in town, Gertrude wielded a certain amount of power. In 1991, when the library was going through renovations and expansions, workers found the banned books walled up in an old chimney.

Gertrude was also not easy to work with. When the original library was being constructed, Gertrude badgered workers and was more disruptive than helpful. She ended up falling from some scaffolding and broke her leg. Gertrude ended up suing the foreman because he didn't tell her to stay off said scaffolding.

Gertrude was also an activist and a member of the National Woman's Party, which played a pivotal role in woman suffrage and eventually gaining the right to vote for women in 1920. Gertrude was on the front lines speaking to politicians, traveling and drafting bills. She also played a significant part in getting the Equal Rights Amendment presented to Congress, which guaranteed legal gender equality for women and men.

In an ironic turn of events, in March 1957, Black upholsterer Samuel Murray was denied entrance to the library because of the color of his skin. It's unsure just how involved Gertrude was, since this took place about nine years before her death. Murray took the library to court, and the board of supervisors and the town council threatened to cut off funds from the library. This drove the trustees to vote— seven to five—to keep the library open. The library became the county's first desegregated library that year because of the Murray incident.

Top: Historic Purcellville Library. *Call number: vc_0004_1706 r, Collection, Rust Archive, Thomas Balch Library, Leesburg, Virginia.*

Bottom: Purcellville Library circa 2023. *Author's collection.*

Gertrude passed away in February 1966, but it seems that she still runs the library from the other side. A librarian by the name of Susie Shackleford went on record with famed Virginia ghost historian L.B. Taylor and told him that one of the most common occurrences in the library is books being thrown from the shelves. These aren't random books, either. These are books that Gertrude herself would have deemed inappropriate for the library.

A shadow has also been seen wandering the inside of the library after dark. When the library was going through its expansion, which would be completed in 1993, workers refused to continue after dark because they would hear footsteps above them. It seems even in death, Gertrude wanted to have a say in the renovation, just as she did when the library first opened.

At one point in her life, Gertrude owned an electric clock. When the library experienced a power outage long after Gertrude's death, the electric clock stayed on. Shackleford recalled that even when she unplugged the clock and removed it from the wall, it was still running.

One of the more concerning incidents happened when Gertrude's portrait had to be removed from the mantel due to water leakage in its usual place. A staffer took the portrait and went to store it in the reference room. However, the reference room was locked. They went to the fire doors, and even those were locked. Fire doors are usually never locked. So the staffer went to get a key. But the effort was fruitless, because even the keys weren't working. At that moment, the staffer looked at the portrait of Gertrude and felt that her eyes were burning a hole into the staffer. This made the staffer feel incredibly nervous, so they called the locksmith. Was Gertrude expressing her disapproval over her portrait being removed? It seems that Gertrude is not just hanging around the Purcellville Library in the afterlife. She's clutching it tightly and hanging on for as long as she can.

CHAPTER 5

CLARKE COUNTY

On Sunday, December 1, 1974, tragedy struck the area near the Mount Weather Emergency Operations Center in Bluemont, Virginia, in Clarke County. It is near Purcellville and about fifty-one miles west of Washington, D.C.

There were ninety-two people on board Trans World Airlines (TWA) Flight 514, including eighty-five passengers and seven crew members. The plane had departed from Indianapolis, Indiana, with a stopover in Columbus, Ohio, and was en route to Ronald Reagan Washington National Airport (DCA). At the time, the East Coast was dealing with severe weather: high winds, rain and snow. The weather and high crosswinds at DCA made it impossible to land on the runway, so the plane was diverted to Dulles. Other planes were also being diverted to Dulles.

As the plane was approaching Dulles, it was cleared for approach at seven thousand feet, but there was confusion as to what "clear to approach" meant at the time. In 1974, there were different definitions for being cleared for landing, and there wasn't a clear meaning for the term that was universal across airports. The plane's pilots thought they could descend, but they couldn't.

Mount Weather has a ridge. Just six weeks before the crash, a United Airlines flight came very close to hitting the ridge, but there was no mention of the ridge in a report by that flight's pilot.

The plane hit the west slope of the ridge, struck the trees and crashed into a rock outcropping. The plane broke apart, and all the passengers were killed. The ridge has since been renamed TWA Ridge.

The crash resulted in three safety enhancements. One was to make it clear what it means to approach and have clearer instructions on procedures. The next was the implementation of a ground proximity warning system that would alert pilots when they were in danger of flying into the ground or some object. The final safety enhancement was the Aviation Safety Reporting System, which documents mistakes that could be made by other pilots. This would have been relevant when the United Airlines flight almost hit that ridge, because had there been a note about that ridge, it could have been avoided by TWA Flight 514.

While the crash site isn't accessible, it seems that activity occurs on the road nearby. Over the years since the crash, odd anomalies have been reported, such as phantom lights, cries and screams, a smoke plume and more. One of the more common stories is about a phantom hitchhiker.

A few decades after the crash, one man shared the story of how he was driving on Blue Ridge Mountain Road, not too far from the crash site memorial, when he saw a pilot walking down the road. The man pulled over and asked the pilot where he was heading. The pilot said he was trying to get to Dulles Airport. The man offered the pilot a ride, and the pilot got into the passenger seat. As the man started driving and asking questions to get to know the pilot, he looked over at the passenger side and saw that the pilot was gone.

Could this phantom pilot still be trying to get to his destination all these years later? It is said that some ghosts stick around due to unfinished business. Could getting to Dulles be this pilot's unfinished business?

Phil Rossi of Old Spirits Investigations visited the crash site area with his wife, Tina. They thought they were at the site for about half an hour. But when they got back to their car, only five minutes had passed.

Rossi and his paranormal partner, Tee Morris, visited the site a bit later. Rossi noted that during the day, the energy around the area is somber and has a sad vibe. But at night, the energy completely changes. When Morris asked the spirits if they should return at night, a voice said, "No."

When Rossi and Morris returned to the area at night, the energy didn't feel good—almost like there was a sense of malcontent. It felt like something didn't want them there but also wanted them there, at the same time, for malicious reasons. They also reported getting interactions on their equipment. The pair heard strange noises in the night, as well as unspecified "weird" occurrences that didn't sit right with either of them. Getting EVPs outdoors is always tricky, but Rossi mentioned that they did get a few pieces of interesting audio.

Like the previous visit, Rossi mentioned that he thought he and Morris were at the site for around thirty to forty-five minutes. But when he checked his device, he was surprised to see that it had only recorded for thirteen minutes. As Rossi reviewed the evidence from the investigation, the feelings of malcontent and the intense vibe came back.

Rossi and Morris eventually returned to the crash site with flowers. They told the spirits of the area that they considered it an honor to tell their story.

Between the interactions that Rossi and Morris experienced and the phantom pilot hitchhiker experiences, it seems that there are souls left behind from the crash that still want their voices heard and still yearn to complete their unfinished business.

PART III

EXPANSE OF NORTHERN VIRGINIA

CHAPTER 6
PRINCE WILLIAM COUNTY

WOODBRIDGE, VIRGINIA

RIPPON LODGE

One of the oldest homes still standing in the Woodbridge area is the Rippon Lodge, built in the early 1700s. The precise date when the house was built is still in question, but it's believed that the foundation was erected around 1725, since it appears in a local survey from 1747, and "1725" is carved into one of the wooden pieces of the foundation. Over its three-hundred-year history, many have owned the house, with various personalities.

But before Rippon Lodge was built, according to a 1993 *Potomac News* article, the land it sits on was considered sacred by the Indigenous community that inhabited the area. In 1725, Richard Blackburn sailed from England to the Americas. He staked out a spot on a high knoll overlooking Neabsco Creek, the Potomac River, meadows and woodland. Blackburn built a home there and named it Rippon Lodge after the town where he grew up: Ripon, in Yorkshire, England. Blackburn and his wife, Mary, had three children: a daughter, Eliza, and two sons, Thomas and William.

Thomas Blackburn was good friends with George Washington, who slept at Rippon Lodge twice, which is one reason people visit the house today. Two Blackburn girls also married into the Washington family. Thomas's daughter Julie Anna married Washington's nephew Bushrod. Then Bushrod's nephew John Augustine married Jane Charlotte Blackburn.

It was so strongly believed that the house was haunted that, in 1911, the *Manassas Journal* and a Richmond newspaper reported that the path for Route 1 was diverted away from the house as a way to keep ghosts from traveling on the main road. The *Manassas Journal* article states, "This house is said to be haunted in so ghostly and sinister fashion that no one will occupy it, and the public road has changed its course to avoid the neighborhood."

The site saw two deaths related to dueling during the eighteenth and nineteenth centuries. One brought the fight right to Rippon Lodge. The duel took place in the Dumfries Cemetery. Because the injured party was a relative of the Blackburn family, he was placed in a wagon and brought to Rippon Lodge, where he bled out and died right in the parlor. Both men are believed to haunt the house, perhaps living with the anguish of unfinished business as their lives were taken too soon.

The second duel occurred in Maryland, since at that point, dueling was illegal in Virginia. Once again, the mortally injured party was taken to Rippon Lodge, and he ended up dying right in the doorway. (Historians are unsure which doorway it was.)

Visitors have claimed to see a bloody print on the floor that was caused by Thomas Blackburn's wife, Christian Scott Blackburn. Mrs. Blackburn shoved a young enslaved girl out of her way. The girl fell to the floor, hit her head on the stone fireplace and died. The child was later buried on the nearby hill. It is reported that the girl haunts the fireplace where she lost her life, and she has also been seen hovering around her resting place.

There is a Blackburn family plot on the property, and it's believed that many of their enslaved were buried with them around the area. After Mrs. Blackburn died in 1815, Rippon Lodge stayed vacant for a number of years before it was bought by George Atkinson, whose family kept the house for over a century. The house was sold in 1911 and once again in 1924 to a judge named Wade Hampton Ellis. He was reported to have quite a vivid imagination, and it's believed some of the ghost stories originated with him. After Ellis's death in 1948, Rippon Lodge found its way back into the Blackburn family when Admiral Richard Blackburn, also known as Black, bought the house. His daughter sold Rippon Lodge to the county in 2000.

A volunteer by the name of LouAnn Dorrier has had her share of ghostly experiences. She reported to InsideNoVa.com that one night, Rippon was hosting a Boy Scout troop for an overnight. Dorrier ran a recorder all night to see what she could capture. The recording revealed a long night of footsteps and doors opening and closing, all while the Boy Scout troop was asleep.

Another night, Dorrier was in the office that's in a cabin behind the house. She saw something walk by, but no one was there. It's a tradition among staff members to say goodnight to Mrs. Christian Blackburn every day, which seems to keep the grumpy old woman at bay. Other staff members have reported having paranormal experiences over the years, so Dorrier isn't alone in her experiences.

The grave of an Occoquan woman by the name of Rose Peters also sits on the property. It is the oldest grave in the cemetery, from the 1600s, long before Richard Blackburn arrived in 1725. Peters was believed to be a woman of a dishonorable nature and ill repute, which seems to mean she was a sinner. Exactly what this meant is unknown; she could have been unbaptized or engaged in activities considered sinful in her time. Her grave was originally located where Interstate 95 would eventually be built. Richard Blackburn arranged to have her grave moved to Rippon Lodge so she wouldn't be buried under the interstate.

DUMFRIES, VIRGINIA

Dumfries in Prince William County is a small town thirty to forty-five minutes south of Washington, D.C., off I-95. If not for the exit sign letting you know you're in Dumfries, you could easily miss it. The town may not be much to look at by modern standards, but during the colonial era, it was one of the most important cities in the area. The first house and warehouse were built in the area in 1731, and the town quickly boomed, specializing in shipped goods in the 1700s and 1800s. Scottish merchants operated out of Dumfries and had it chartered in 1749.

THE WEEMS-BOTTS MUSEUM

The Weems-Botts Museum is one of the oldest houses in Dumfries. It's named after two of its owners: Mason Locke "Parson" Weems and Benjamin Botts. It's believed to have been built around 1750 and was originally used as a warehouse and poorhouse by a local church.

In 1798, Parson Weems purchased the house. Weems was an author and bookseller, and he was one of the most notable writers who drove the myth of George Washington and the cherry tree, in which Washington declares,

Weems-Botts Museum circa 2023. *Author's collection.*

"I cannot tell a lie." He wrote biographies of other Founding Fathers for the rest of his career.

In 1869, Richard Merchant purchased the house, where he lived with his wife, Annie, and two daughters, Mary (better known as Mamie) and Violet. Mamie suffered from epilepsy during a time when the condition wasn't well understood. She was locked in her room, unable to leave the house for fear of having a seizure in public. The house and her room were her prison until she passed away in 1906 at the age of twenty-three. Richard died that same year. Violet, who had moved away, returned home to care for her mother until Annie's death in 1952. Violet continued to live in the house until she passed of old age in 1968. The house fell into disrepair and was set to be demolished until it was saved by the town. It opened as a museum in 1976.

While the house was going through renovations, strange occurrences began. Books would fly off the shelves of an added bookshelf as if they were being thrown across the room.

Over the years, there have been multiple reports of ghost sightings at the house—some consider it the second most haunted house in Virginia. Civil War soldiers have reportedly been seen in the park behind the house as well as in nearby cemeteries, even though the war has long been over. Ghost hunters have also heard a child's voice and picked it up on several pieces of equipment. Violet's room has been a center of activity, with a window opening and closing by itself with no explanation.

It is believed that the Merchant family never left the house after their deaths, especially Mamie. Much of the noise in the house seems to come from her room. Since she spent most of her life there, likely experiencing seizures alone, surely the terrifying experience embedded itself in the room. Footsteps and screams are heard from the room, and curtains move when there are no windows open. Mamie's spirit has also been seen, as reported during a visit to the house by a Boy Scout troop. During their visit, the Boy Scouts saw Mamie sitting in her rocking chair, looking out at the outside world.

Occoquan, Virginia

Occoquan, Virginia, about twenty miles south of Washington, D.C., is considered one of the most charming historic small towns in the United States.

In July 1608, John Smith explored the Occoquan River and the surrounding area. He was immediately welcomed by the Doeg tribe at their settlement of Tauxenent. More Europeans would make their way into the area, like William Fitzhugh, who had tanyards over at the Occoquan River falls. When he passed away in 1700, he left the tanyards to his heirs.

Occoquan was established as a town in 1734, making it one of the oldest towns in the area. It started off as mainly warehouses for tobacco, its residents' main source of income. In 1735, Valentine Peyton established his tobacco business.

The town certainly started to thrive in 1758, when John Ballendine purchased twenty acres of land and established the iron foundry, a sawmill, a gristmill, bakehouses and various other business on the banks of the Occoquan River. Yet Ballendine wasn't able to enjoy these businesses for very long, as he lost them to foreclosure in 1765. According to historical records, he was someone with great ideas—often described as a visionary—but he didn't do well with money, and he was often late making payments.

By 1765, the area had started to boom, and people were moving there in hopes of making their fortune. The first automated gristmill was the Merchant's Mill, which functioned for about 175 years until it was destroyed in a fire.

After Nathanial Ellicott purchased Ballendine's foreclosed properties, he and his associates officially founded the town of Occoquan on thirty-one acres. They laid out the streets, built an automated gristmill and constructed a footbridge to go over the Occoquan River.

Artist's rendering of a bloody fight between Union soldiers and a Confederate soldier as it appeared in *Harper's Weekly* on February 15, 1862. *Library of Congress.*

In 1776, members of the Occoquan Baptist Church petitioned the Virginia Convention for religious freedom. Occoquan wouldn't be recognized as a town until 1805.

During the Civil War, Occoquan was not exempt from its share of fights. In 1862, General Wade Hampton had his headquarters at the Hammill Hotel, which may have been one of the first brick buildings in the town; it still stands today.

Today, while the tobacco warehouses and gristmills no longer exist, the town has not only survived but also thrived. There are multiple small shops and businesses in Occoquan, including art galleries, antique shops and restaurants serving unique local dishes. Occoquan has become quite the tourist spot, having established itself as a small-town getaway by the river for Washington, D.C. tourists. Today, parts of Rockledge Mansion and gristmills still stand at the end of Mill Street.

Occoquan is a town where people have worked hard throughout history. The people of the past were very much invested in their buildings, which could explain why there are so many ghosts in such a small section of road of the town.

Rockledge Mansion

Sitting at 440 Mill Street, Rockledge Mansion was built in 1758 by John Ballendine, one of the founders of the town as we know it. It is certainly one of the most resilient houses in the area, having gone through significant damage as it witnessed major historical events that created the United States. Ballendine worked with George Washington to improve the infrastructure of Virginia by building canals and making other improvements involving the nearby rivers.

After Quaker Nathanial Ellicott purchased Ballendine's properties in 1765, he put wood siding over the rock, which was a fashionable and popular choice at the time. Ellicott also added a kitchen. The wood siding would last well into the 1800s. Ellicott left Occoquan and moved to Alexandria in 1861, and the Janney family purchased the house in 1829; they owned it until 1929.

But over the years, owning Rockledge was not a picnic for the Janneys. In 1836, the harbor fell victim to immense water pollution, preventing ships from reaching the mill. Other areas like Dumfries were also affected by similar issues, and eventually the siltation, made Neabsco Bay and Creek unnavigable. Occoquan was hit hard by the migration of the farming industry heading West, the loss of its mail route and railroads diverting trade away from the area.

The head of the Janney family, Joseph T., found himself in trouble when he allowed local men to erect a flagpole at Rockledge, which flew a pennant depicting Abraham Lincoln and his running mate, Hannibal Hamlin. In 1860, the Prince William militia arrived at Rockledge and chopped down the flagpole. Janney protested the action, and Union sympathizers joined in. Who knew that the Civil War would start a year later? The house ended up surviving the Civil War, miraculously enough.

In 1902, the Consolidated Stone Quarry conducted blasting across the river, sending boulders flying toward Rockledge and the surrounding houses and causing significant foundational issues as well as damage.

By the time the Janney family sold Rockledge to Fred Almon Barnes in 1929, the house was in horrific shape. Throughout his life, Barnes worked on repairing and restoring Rockledge, which project he wouldn't see completed in his lifetime. He left the house to his son Laurence Barnes. Laurence and his wife were able to get the house designated a historic site. But they had to flee the home in 1960 due to more damage caused by blasting projects. Their attempts to get compensated for the damage were not successful.

Rockledge Mansion. *Library of Congress.*

The house stood vacant until Donald Sonner bought it in 1970, wanting to restore it as a Christmas present for his wife. But before the Sonners could move in, a burglar broke into the house, then set it on fire to cover his tracks. The Sonners' insurance company refused to compensate them since they weren't living in the house yet.

The Sonners ran out of money to work on the house, and they sold it to Ronald and Joy Houghton in 1982. The Houghtons had more success with the house. They cleaned, repaired and restored Rockledge and also lived in it. For a time, they even ran a bed-and-breakfast in the house; then their son Lance ran the house as an event center.

Rockledge experienced damage once again from Hurricane Irene, as well as an earthquake, in 2011.

The paranormal happenings reported at Rockledge are interesting. The most prominent story is that a Confederate soldier haunts the mansion. Occoquan did see its share of action during the Civil War, and there doesn't seem to be a rule in the world of hauntings that all ghosts have to be attached to the property they haunt. Perhaps this Confederate soldier found comfort in Rockledge and decided to make it his home. According to legend, a young woman haunts the area where the ballroom is now, known as the White Lady.

Vayne Konstantine, born in Occoquan and a lifelong resident, gave me more insight into the legend of the White Lady. She can be seen wearing a white gown and pacing either through the top floor of Rockledge or in the direction of what's known as the Spot.

Konstantine told me,

> *The legend goes that the White Lady was a young woman who was having a secret affair with the mansion owner at that time, and he had built a secret tunnel under the mansion in the basement from where she lived (the Spot) to the mansion. He'd sneak her up the small staircase into a secret room to carry out said affair. He promised her he'd leave his family for her and they'd run off together to start a new life. He ended up not keeping his promise and left town with his own family, without her. Feeling abandoned and distraught, the young woman committed suicide in her bedroom, where the workers of a home goods store called Tastefully Yours would leave a candle lit every night in remembrance of her. How much of this is true, I'll never know. I speculate most of it isn't.*

But then Konstantine said,

> *But I will say this; the one time I went down into the mansion's basement to collect one of the store's mischievous cats, I saw an area against the wall that looked like it was bricked up differently from the rest of the wall, like there was a tunnel there once. For what it was used or what it actually was, I don't know and have never been able to find out.*

Konstantine eventually found herself working at Rockledge and having a few interesting experiences.

> *I've been working at 13 Magickal Moons (the local witch shop) for a few years, and we had just moved our shop into Rockledge Mansion. My best friend, Avery, and I had the mansion to ourselves at around midnight one night as we were putting all of the herb jars for the shop in alphabetical order in the top far left room (unknown to us at the time, one of the most haunted spots in the house). As we were working, we started to hear very heavy boot steps walking from the far right room toward the room we were currently in. Both me and Avery stopped what we were doing to look at each other in shock; we even stopped breathing. We then peeked down the dark hallway to see who (or what) it was, considering that we*

> *were locked inside the mansion by ourselves. After seeing that no one was there, we dropped what we were doing and quickly left the mansion. This would be my first—but far from the last—paranormal experience inside Rockledge Mansion.*

It seems that more is happening at Rockledge than encounters with the famous Confederate soldier, and it's worthy of further investigation. Konstantine continued with another story:

> *The encounter I will never forget was when the downstairs still was set up to look historical and the parlor room (bottom far right room) had a grand piano in front of the side window, with an antique vanity tilting mirror on top. I was alone that night, in the process of closing up. As I was walking down the main stairs to leave, I noticed the parlor room door was open at the bottom of the stairs, which I found unusual. As I got down there and I began to pull the door shut, I saw movement out of the corner of my eye in the dark room. I slowly lift my eyes up and see in the reflection of the mirror atop the piano: a lady sitting down at the piano bench and looking up and at me through the mirror. She was a young Caucasian woman dressed in black, gray and dark blue historical clothing of possibly around the late 1700s or early 1800s. She had dark hair and almost grayish pale skin with dark, hollowed eyes. I stood there in complete shock and, I won't lie, even a little bit of fear. I had never before seen a spirit so clearly, and I didn't know how to feel. As I stood there in disbelief, an overwhelming feeling of sadness, betrayal and loneliness overcame me. I blinked once and she was gone, like she had never been there. I'm not sure if she was channeling her emotions through me to "understand" her, but I felt no malice or evil intent. This also would not be my last time seeing her.*

I did ask Konstantine about the story of the Confederate soldier that's been reported at the house. She said,

> *In regards to how the town's history contributes to its haunted reputation, this story is a good example. A story was told that I can't find accurate information to confirm: the mansion was used as a hospice during the Civil War, and thus that is how the Confederate soldier's ghost came to be inside the mansion. It was said that during the time the mansion was a hospice, a Confederate soldier was taken there for a fatal wound. In the middle of the night, the soldier attempted to escape and desert the war, knowing he'd*

be thrown right back in if he survived his wounds. He fell down the main staircase during his escape and ended up bleeding to death; as a result, his spirit haunts the staircase. I'm also not sure how much of this information is accurate due to the mansion's recorded history being very vague.

THE TOMBSTONE AT THE MILL HOUSE MUSEUM

The Mill House Museum dates to 1765, and it served as the administrative office for Merchants Mill (established in 1757), believed to be one of the first automated gristmills in the United States and owned by Quaker Nathanial Ellicott. The space was converted from the original ironworks complex that John Ballendine lost in 1765. The mill and attached ironworks were essential during the Revolutionary War, providing grain from the mill and iron from the furnaces for the Patriots.

Ruins of Merchant's Mill and Mill House. *Library of Congress.*

The mill continued to be used until 1924. Unfortunately, a generator fire destroyed the structure. But the smaller Mill House survived. However, it wasn't well taken care of, and it almost collapsed into itself.

The Alexandria Water Company purchased the Mill House in the mid-twentieth century when construction started on the Occoquan dams. The Mill House was used as an office space once more. When the Fairfax Water Authority, now known as Fairfax Water, moved in, it gave the structure to the Town of Occoquan.

Presently, the Town of Occoquan has leased the Mill House to the Occoquan Historical Society; it is now used as a museum.

There is a tombstone on display at the Mill House Museum. It was discovered by workmen who were excavating the bulkhead along the Occoquan River behind Madigan's Waterfront Restaurant. Freezing cold to the touch, the tombstone dates to 1893. If you're brave enough to touch the tombstone, you may feel a chill go down your spine.

Madigan's Waterfront

This restaurant is known as not only a great place to get a bite to eat but also a spot to find some ghosts. Madigan's is a boathouse that was converted into a restaurant. Rachael Bright's ghost tour visits Madigan's, and she was able to tell me that it's home to the spirits of two little girls. One died from the Spanish flu and the other from scarlet fever. Restaurant guests have accidentally bumped into a child, only to find there's not a child around; seen a chair being turned around; and heard mysterious knocking sounds.

206 Mill Street

Forever Young Med Spa sits at 206 Mill Street, one of many businesses that have resided in the home over the years. While the current structure was built in 1916, there are stories about an eighteenth-century structure at the address where shows and circus performances took place. Reportedly, the spirit of the girl named Charlotte will rearrange merchandise when it arrives.

Top: Madigan's Waterfront Restaurant. *Author's collection.*

Bottom: 206 Mill Street. *Author's collection.*

301 MILL STREET

The building on 301 Mill Street in Occoquan, Virginia, has a fascinating history. It was constructed in 1780, per the historical marker on the building. By 1810, it had been serving as an inn or a tavern throughout its history and had been reconstructed a few times.

According to local legend, the ghost of a Native American man who died inside haunts the building. This man was a member of the Doeg tribe. Because Indigenous Americans were being driven out West, this man was the only member of his tribe left in Occoquan. Some variations of the story set it in the late 1700s, when there was a more harmonious arrangement between local tribes and settlers in Occoquan. The Native American man was employed by a tavern owner, and he started an affair with the tavern owner's wife. One night, the tavern owner heard the man sneaking out of the bedroom and walking down the building's wooden steps. He shot the man as he was coming onto the last step.

The paranormal activity surrounding this Indigenous man includes him appearing in the smoke of the fireplace. Over the years, the building has been reconstructed, and little of the original building from the 1700s remains except for the fireplace. The man's reflection has also been seen in the large mirror in the women's bathroom. He is described as tall with long black hair.

When the building was occupied by the Occoquan Inn, staff seemed to be very willing to share their paranormal experiences. The activity centered on young women, who had various experiences, including feeling like someone was blowing on their neck. One staff member reported that often, when she was closing for the evening, she saw someone out of the corner of her eye. When she turned to get a better look, she found that no one was there.

D'Rocco's Italian Restaurant. *Author's collection.*

According to another story, the town clerk came into the Occoquan Inn and needed to use the restroom. As she was standing in front of the sink, she reported feeling a breeze on her legs—and then an unseen entity grabbed her ankles.

Another incident took place at closing time. The manager on duty for the evening was going through the building to make sure all the lights and fans were turned off. When the men's and women's restrooms are cleaned, the doors are left open afterward. After checking the women's restroom, the manager went to check the men's and found that the door was shut. When she checked to see if the door was locked (it can only be locked from the outside), she found it was unlocked, but it was as if someone was holding it shut. The manager was able to push the door open enough to get her hand and arm through to turn off the light. However, the door once again was pushed shut, and the manager got her arm bruised.

Today, D'Rocco's Italian Restaurant occupies the space, with the Tap Room in its basement. It's unknown whether the current staff of the restaurant have had similar paranormal experiences; only time will tell for sure.

302 MILL STREET

According to the historical marker on the building, 302 Mill Street was built in 1860. The building has been home to many businesses, including Leary's Lumber and Hardware Store and the Golden Goose. At the time of this writing, Curate occupies the space. A ghost is said to appear by the old sales counter that can be seen from the front window. But this phenomenon only happens after business hours. Perhaps an old clerk from years past is counting the money from a busy day of sales.

302 Mill Street. *Author's collection.*

305 Mill Street

Puzzle Palooza currently sits at 305 Mill Street. After opening their business in 2013 with the intention to sell puzzles for all ages, owner Donna Carleton and her partner Holly VandenHeuvel soon started to notice strange happenings there.

One of the incidents involved VandenHeuvel's son, who was manning the shop that day. Carleton called him to tell him to close for the day, since it was raining and business was slow. VandenHeuvel's son told Carlton that they had a ghost: the lights kept flickering, the Internet was going in and out and the door had opened several times by itself. He'd made sure that the door was shut properly, and yet it kept opening. During the phone conversation, Carleton heard a bang. When she asked the son what it was, he said it was a puzzle that had fallen off the shelf by itself.

VandenHeuvel also had a strange encounter. One morning, she came into work and placed her lunch in the refrigerator. When she came for her food at lunchtime, she was surprised to see that four puzzle boxes were set end-to-end in front of the refrigerator door. The boxes had not been there before.

On hearing this, Carleton decided to conduct an experiment. She left a floor puzzle out with only a few pieces left to be completed over on one side. When she returned the next day, the puzzle was complete. The experiment continued a few more times, and each time, the puzzle was complete the next day.

So Carleton called Kay Pietrewicz, a local paranormal investigator who ran Haunted Occoquan, which features ghost tours. Pietrewicz conducted a communication session with the ghost using dowsing rods and recorded the event. She discovered that there was indeed a ghost at the Puzzle Pallooza. He was a seven-year-old boy named Tad whose father worked in Occoquan, and he apparently didn't have the use of his left arm.

307 Mill Street

At 307 Mill Street, where Gift & Gather currently resides, a flickering light has reportedly been seen in the windows in the early morning hours. It is believed that a female spirit is responsible, as she is holding a candle and walking throughout the building.

Left: 309 Mill Street. *Author's collection.*

Above: The Spot at 406 Mill Street. *Author's collection.*

309 MILL STREET

Today a spot for retail outlets, 309 Mill Street is the former location of a funeral parlor. There are reports of footsteps being heard in the building even though no one is there.

406 MILL STREET

The Spot on Mill Street was once occupied by the business Tastefully Yours and is connected with Rockledge Mansion. The story goes that the White Lady who has been seen at Rockledge was a woman who was having an affair with the mansion owner. To better accommodate their secret meetings, he built a tunnel under the mansion that led to her home, which is where the Spot is today. The owner would take the woman up the staircase and into a secret room to proceed with the affair. He promised the young woman that he would leave his family for her. But when he instead left town with his family, leaving the young woman behind, she committed suicide. It is alleged that employees at this address, both past and present, would light candles in her memory.

313 MILL STREET

The Loft Gallery at 313 Mill Street was once the home of the town general store. Today, it hosts about twenty artists who have a plethora of different artistic styles and abilities. It is certainly a hub for creativity and inspiration. The bricks that were used to build the location were made in England and were originally used as ballast for a ship.

Perhaps between the historic bricks and the arts, paranormal activity was almost guaranteed to happen. Visitors to the Loft have reported hearing floors creaking with mysterious unseen footsteps, doors closing on their own and a painting flying off the wall. One witness also reported seeing a mist floating through the gallery early one morning.

408 MILL STREET

Local Color Gallery and Boutique is the art gallery of Rachael Bright, who also runs Occoquan Spirits, a local ghost tour with a focus on restaurants and the option to enjoy cocktails along the way. When Bright first moved in, she encountered the spirit of a seven-year-old boy named Tad who stole her red smock and wore it like a Superman cape.

When I spoke to Bright on the phone, she shared with me that she has had the ability to see spirits since she was six years old. When it comes to young Tad, Bright told me that he is trying to locate his family.

312 COMMERCE STREET

The building at 312 Commerce Street is home to a plant nursery called Leaf and Moss. According to locals, the house is home to a spirit that unscrews the lightbulbs and messes with the thermostat.

According to the real estate listing for the house, it dates to the 1700s, but Zillow states it was built in 1901. It is quite possible that, like the other buildings in Occoquan, the original structure was rebuilt over the years. It was owned by the same family from the 1930s until it was sold in 2021. Perhaps this spirit was a relative of the family that owned the house before, and they weren't ready to say goodbye.

201 UNION STREET

The town well was once located in a courtyard at 201 Union Street that previously existed before development went up around it. The spirit that

Left: 313 Mill Street. *Author's collection.*

Right: 408 Mill Street. *Author's collection.*

312 Commerce Street. *Author's collection.*

201 Union Street. *Author's collection.*

204 Washington Street. *Author's collection.*

haunts the area is said to prefer quiet as much as possible—so much so that anything noisy that enters the former well area is silenced by an unseen entity, including wind chimes.

204 Washington Street

Built in 1910, 204 Washington Street serves as a retail store today. It is said that there are several poltergeists in the building that often make their presence known during the day. The use of the word *poltergeist* in this context is interesting, because paranormal investigators and parapsychologists define poltergeists as a manifestation of the mind. Poltergeists are usually prominent in young women going through puberty, with its hormonal surges and both external and internal stress; it's believed that poltergeists are external manifestations of that stress in the form of objects moving by themselves.

Brentsville, Virginia

A little over forty-one miles southeast of Washington, D.C., is Brentsville, Virginia, a hamlet of Prince William County. Brentsville was established in 1820, and it was the county seat. The area was used to train Confederate soldiers before they went off to war. The area, like most of Virginia, was heavily affected by numerous Civil War battles. Confederate soldiers from Virginia, of all ranks, came home to find their homes and farms destroyed. Homes and churches that weren't destroyed served as hospitals for the sick and wounded. Other buildings, like the county clerk's office, were torn down and the bricks were used for camp chimneys.

On October 14, 1863, the Battle of Bristoe Station was fought about three miles west of Brentsville. Union general John Buford's cavalry was posted in Brentsville to protect the Federal supply train.

The town of Brentsville was once busy—as not only the county seat but also an important town for both sides during the Civil War. Today, the town is quiet, with a somber mood, as if it is reflecting on what took place there during one of the most important moments in U.S. history. And surely there are spirits left behind to tell us their stories.

Brentsville Courthouse and Historic Center in Bristow, Virginia, is a twenty-eight-acre property with several archaeological sites and buildings, including the Haislip-Hall House, the courthouse, a jail, a schoolhouse and a Union church.

Brentsville Courthouse and Gallows

The Brentsville Courthouse was built in 1822. Behind the courthouse is the gallows where thirteen people were executed. All but one was African American, and two of them were enslaved women. Gallows weren't often used for execution in the nineteenth century, so this was a rather unique, if not barbaric, feature of the town of Brentsville. Whippings and lashings were all part of the theater of public execution. The gallows were not a permanent fixture, as they were constructed right before a public execution and taken down after. White prisoners were tried and convicted in circuit courts, while enslaved and free Blacks were tried in county courts, which often used capital punishment. As the gallows was right in the window, possibly in the prisoner's view, it loomed as a reminder of what was to come should they be found guilty and sentenced to death.

In 1820, an enslaved woman named Katy was killed by her master, Gerald Mason, who was a distant cousin of Founding Father George Mason. He was taken to trial and later acquitted. Thirty years later, in 1850, an enslaved woman named Agness was asked by Mason to get the hatchet and split some firewood. According to Agness's testimony, Mason looked at her the same way he did Katy before he killed her. Agness wasn't going to take any chances. When Mason fell asleep, she swung the hatchet at his head and killed him. It is believed that Mason attempted to force himself on her and held her baby over a pot of hot oil as a coercion method. Agness claimed she was pregnant, and it was illegal to execute a pregnant woman in Virginia. However, after two months in jail, it was determined that Agness wasn't pregnant, and she was executed. According to another variation of the story, a doctor made the claim that Agness wasn't pregnant without checking, prompting her execution.

The courthouse roof was torn off during the Civil War, and many county records were lost, destroyed or taken by Union soldiers as souvenirs. The history of the jail and courthouse is riddled with problematic stories.

When it comes to the paranormal, people have reported seeing Agness's ghost in the courthouse and the gallows area. Given that Agness's story is

Right: Brentsville Courthouse gallows area. *Author's collection.*

Below: Brentsville Courthouse interior. *Author's collection.*

an example of racism and the gross miscarriage of justice, perhaps Agness isn't present just to prove that she existed but to serve as a reminder of the horrific crimes committed against the enslaved in the nineteenth century.

BRENTSVILLE JAIL

The Brentsville Jail was also built in 1822. Inmates were housed there as they awaited trial. Unfortunately, not just criminals were held there. Free Black people and enslaved people were confined to the jail after being illegally captured or rebelling against their masters. Women were also jailed in the building, as well as those who suffered from mental illness. Politicians who disagreed with major leaders also found themselves behind bars. It seemed that what should have been a place to hold criminals was abused to make the marginalized suffer. If an inmate was found guilty and the sentence wasn't death by hanging, they were transferred to a prison in Richmond, Virginia. After the county seat moved to Manassas, the building was used as a school called the Prince William Academy from 1897 to 1905, then as a dormitory and office space. Today, it is a museum with powerful exhibits on African American history and the jail's involvement in oppressing Black people.

One of the most famous ghost stories tied to the jail is that of attorney James F. Clark. He was accused of having an affair with sixteen-year-old Fanny Fewell, who was the daughter of a prominent Manassas citizen. When Fanny ran off with Clark, who had also abandoned his wife and child, he was accused of kidnapping. Clark returned to Brentsville to clear his name and was arrested instead. His trial was one of the most popular media stories of the 1800s in Virginia. He continued to proclaim his innocence until August 30, 1872, when Fanny's brother Lucien went to the jail, stuck his pistol between the bars and shot Clark dead in his cell. At Lucien's trial, it took the jury only five minutes to declare him not guilty. The courtroom burst into applause. Lucien had his day in court; Clark didn't.

Today, the jail has become known as a paranormal hotspot. Paranormal investigators and thrill seekers have caught the infamous sayings, "Get out" and "Don't turn out the lights" on their audio recorders. Shadows have also been spotted and objects thrown at visitors. Could this be the ghost of James F. Clark trying to advocate for his innocence—or simply getting people to leave him alone as he waits for his day in court that will never come?

Right: Brentsville Jail. *Author's collection.*

Below: Brentsville jail cell where James F. Clark was killed. *Author's collection.*

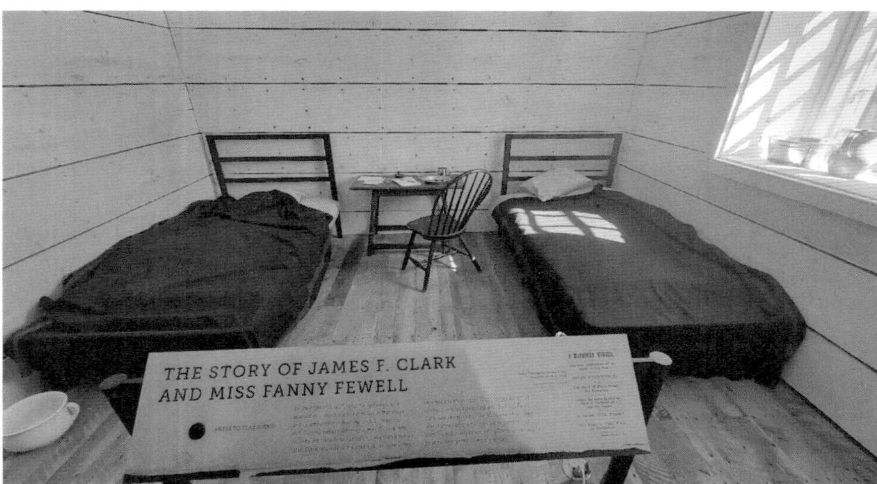

Ghost Hunters TV Show

Season 9, episode 5 of *Ghost Hunters* brought Jason Hawes, Grant Wilson, Steve Gonsalves, Dave Tango and Kris Williams to the Brentsville courthouse and jail. As the historian for the case, Williams reported that full-bodied apparitions, moving objects and cold spots had been experienced on the property. The cold spots also included cold bursts of air indoors with no source.

Residents reported activity in the courthouse dating back sixty years, including faces in the windows in the judge's office, and said they could see someone looking down from the second-story balcony. Some people said it was a gentleman; others said they saw the outline of a face. Witnesses also reported seeing a Black woman's face looking out from the jail door.

When the TAPS team investigated, Jason immediately noted a thermal hit on the camera when entering the old jail. The thermal hit was in the shape of a person, and it almost seemed like the image was burned into the camera. On the second floor, they kept hearing footsteps, as if someone was in the next room. Then the sound moved and was above them, in the attic—but once again, nothing was there.

When Steve Gonsalves and Dave Tango investigated the first-floor cell where Clark was killed, it seemed that Steve started to hear ringing in his ears and head. Dave concluded that perhaps this was a residual haunting and Steve was experiencing one of the last things Clark heard before he died.

Haislip-Hall House

The Haislip-Hall House was built in 1853. It was moved from a location on Linton Hill Road in 2000. Confederate veteran Samuel Haislip built the house in 1850 for his wife and seven children. The Haislip family owned two slaves, and that number eventually grew to eleven enslaved at the Haislip Farm, some living in the house and some in other structures. The house was built with logs and cedar siding and had two bedrooms. With two parents and seven children, plus slaves, the house certainly was busy around the clock.

After the building was relocated, it went through restoration from 2007 to 2008. The area was crafted to resemble a farm in 1850s Virginia and give visitors a look into history.

Haislip-Hall House. *Author's collection.*

Tee Morris took me to the Haislip-Hall House since during a previous visit, he had some weird experiences and got hits on his equipment. As I ran my equipment—including a Phasmabox, which runs on sounds through my laptop—I caught nothing out of the ordinary except for the word *eleven* when I asked how many people were with us, as well as a chant that almost sounded like a children's song.

Given the house's history of seeing the Civil War and then being relocated, is it possible spirits tied to the house went along for the ride? Or perhaps spirits already present at the current location found themselves a place to call home.

CHAPTER 7
STAFFORD COUNTY

The history of Stafford is turbulent, with much of it centered on European colonial and Indigenous communities. The Patawomeck and Manahoac tribes populated the area in great numbers. In fact, Captain John Smith set foot in Stafford after sailing on the Potomac from Jamestown. Pocahontas was abducted in 1613 by English sea captain Samuel Argall in an attempt to bargain for the freedom of English settlers.

In 1664, Stafford County was formally established from Westmoreland County, and it was divided into two parishes, Overwharton and Chotank. During the Colonial period, Stafford's flour mills, tobacco plantations, ironworks and fisheries significantly supported Great Britain. George Washington lived in Stafford from age six to nineteen, and he remains one of the town's most famous residents.

As Civil War swept through Virginia, Stafford played host to multiple Civil War hospitals and encampments. It was a logistical and transportation center for both sides. However, Stafford ultimately ended up hosting 200,000 soldiers of the Union Army of the Potomac. The civilians of Stafford had no choice but to leave their homes. The population of the town didn't recover until well into the twentieth century, in the 1940s.

The population of Stafford County was just over five thousand in 2020.

AQUIA CHURCH

Aquia Church is one of those places that catches the eye in such a way that it's difficult to turn away from it. There's just something about the old structure that beckons people, especially teens and young adults, to come learn more about it. Of course, any old structure is sure to have ghost stories and urban legends surrounding it. During the Halloween season, security around the old church is amplified to protect it from thrill seekers and anyone interested in encountering a ghost. The spot has often been used by teens for a "rite of passage" form of hazing, as well as by brave young men who bring their dates in hopes of playing the brave knight protecting the damsel in distress.

When Stafford County was established, there were three churches. One was the Overwharton Parish, later called Potomac Church, the largest church in the area. Aquia Church was named after the nearby creek and established around 1664–67; it is one of the longest-running congregations in the United States. The original structure burned down before 1700, and a small wooden chapel was built in its place.

Back in the eighteenth century, church attendance was required, otherwise one would be fined. Potomac Church was difficult to reach, due to its distance from the main road. Aquia's wooden church, which was about forty-four years old by this time, was easier to get to, and church leaders in the area met and decided to invest in a more robust construction of Aquia Church to meet the demands of the town.

Construction of today's structure started in 1751. However, a fire in 1754 set the completion of the project back. Heartbreakingly, the church was just three days away from completion when the fire hit. It would take another three years to build Aquia Episcopal Church, which was completed in 1757 and constructed in the shape of a Greek cross. The more well-known members of the church include Thomas Jefferson and George Mason. George Washington had ties with several church members. The original windows from 1757 are still on the church today.

One of the most harrowing stories surrounding Aquia Church is the tragic tale of a woman who was murdered in the building's belfry. It is believed that during the Revolutionary War, a woman was chased down by either a single highwayman or several men. It was a violent struggle, and her body was hidden in the belfry. The church wasn't in use at the time, and it would be years before the woman's skeleton was found, with her golden blonde hair still intact. There were also bloodstains from where the woman was murdered that couldn't be cleaned up and wouldn't disappear until the concrete floor was laid in the church in the early 1900s.

During the 1700s, it was reported that parishioners wouldn't go into the church at night, as it seemed like the woman's murder was being replayed night after night. Footsteps running up and down the stairs of the belfry were heard, cries and screams of a violent struggle pulsed through listening ears and the apparition of a frightened woman was seen in the windows.

Amid the Civil War, Aquia Church stood witness to its events. In 1862, Confederate soldier William Fitzhugh was running a scouting mission with another soldier when they came upon the church and decided to go inside and rest. The pair knew the ghost story about the church, but they were too exhausted to care. They fell asleep in the pews. During the night, the pair were awakened to loud footsteps as well as whistling to the tune of "The Campbells Are Coming." Fitzhugh looked out the window to see a Union regiment heading in their direction. The pair leapt out the window behind the church and got away.

According to another story, a socialite who spent her summers in Stafford back in the 1920s wanted to check out the ghosts for herself. She couldn't get any of the male employees to accompany her to the church, especially since she wanted to go late at night. The socialite managed to find two scientists in Washington, D.C., who were willing to go with her. On the night of their arrival, the socialite walked into the dark church and immediately felt a strong hand strike her, slapping her in the face. The two scientists ran in and searched the church, only to find no other people around.

The Witches Pond

Behind the Crucifix Monument along US 1 in Stafford County is the Brent Family Cemetery, the final resting place for many who were involved in the first settlement of English Roman Catholics in Virginia. The cemetery is owned by the St. William of York Catholic Church, and the oldest grave dates to 1681. Five generations of the Brent family are buried by the pond. The Brent family moved from Baltimore to Virginia to escape religious intolerance and found a new home near Aquia Creek. The Brent family was gifted about thirty thousand acres by King James II, which was technically not his land to give.

Catholics thrived in the area with the ability to freely practice their religion. The population grew to over two hundred. Eventually, though, the community waned and disappeared. It was rediscovered in 1897 when the lost community of Aquia was found again with the discovery of the cemetery.

In the cemetery, one tombstone serves as a tribute to Spanish Jesuits who were massacred by the local Native Americans in 1571. Apparently, an ancestor of the Brents was among those killed.

In 1930, artist Georg J. Lober created the Crucifix Monument in honor of the first English Roman Catholic settlement in Virginia. In 1933, the Catholic Archdiocese of Richmond had a stone altar built in honor of the Brent family. The St. William of York Catholic Church holds mass in the Brent Family Cemetery annually in honor of the Brents.

On November 7, 1998, a hunter found the skeletal remains of a woman about four hundred feet from the pond. The skeleton was covered by fallen leaves, and medical examiners believed that it had been at that spot for around a year. The deceased was believed to be between twenty-five and forty-five years old. She had brown hair in braids and was wearing pantyhose, a Redskins shirt, shorts and blue jeans. (The shorts and jeans combination is certainly interesting.) Her shoe size was eight and a half, and she was wearing canvas platforms with buckles. Her height was between 5'8" and 5'11". Detectives also found a yellow metal earring shaped like a leaf, a pair of dark brown oval-shaped sunglasses, a small plastic teddy bear trinket, a gold ring with black stones and a black onyx ring with a pentagram design.

The mystery woman was named the Stafford County Jane Doe. She has yet to be identified. A clay recreation was made of her face as well.

Legend has it that in the eighteenth century, villagers in Stafford put an alleged witch to death. The execution happened in the woods near a swampy pond near the Aquia Creek. After the alleged witch was killed, her body was thrown into the pond.

Granted, there are no records of a witch ever being put to death in Stafford during Colonial times. However, witchcraft was very much feared at that time. So it's quite possible this story served as a warning to those who have been taken in by the allure of witchcraft.

So where do ghosts fit into all of this? Witnesses claim that the pond turns blood red every spring. There are also reports of a woman hovering over the pond. She has also been seen by the foot path as well as hovering near an altar, which is commonly misidentified as a ritualistic table.

Those who visit the area at night have also heard splashing in the pond, like a body is being tossed into it. Screams have been heard that get closer and closer to the listener in the darkness.

Today, the pond and about seventy-five acres of woods around the area are privately owned. In 2015, the owner said that the Witches Pond lore has been rather annoying for him because it has resulted in unwelcome visitors and trespassers.

Between the legend of Witches Pond and the mystery of the Stafford County Jane Doe, the area has certainly garnered a reputation for being spooky as well as disturbing.

Part IV

Along the Border

CHAPTER 8
FAIRFAX COUNTY

Fairfax County was established in 1742 from Prince William County as its own county. But before it was settled by the English, the area was occupied by the Algonquian-speaking Doeg tribe. One of the area's first foreign visitors was Captain John Smith himself, around 1608, who documented the activities of the Doeg people. By 1670, English settlers had driven out the Doeg people, who moved into Maryland.

Fairfax County was named after Thomas Fairfax, sixth Lord Fairfax of Cameron, proprietor of the Northern Neck. The name Fairfax comes from an old English word meaning "blond hair." One of the most famous residents of Fairfax County is none other than George Washington himself. Fairfax County is where his beloved family homestead, Mount Vernon, is located.

During World War II, the county saw substantial growth due to the federal government expanding rapidly. The area went from rural farmland to a suburban area. Fairfax County is still one of the bigger counties in Northern Virginia, spanning over four hundred square miles. That means there are plenty of spirits ready to tell their stories.

Burke, Virginia

Huldah Coffer House

About seven miles west of Springfield and a little over six miles south of Fairfax is the Huldah Coffer House, today known as the Woods Community Center in Burke, Virginia. The house was built around 1876 for Huldah Virginia Simpson Coffer on land owned by the Coffer family. The house was also known as Locust Hill. The Coffers were prominent in the area and well known. Huldah was married to Joshua Coffer, who was twenty-five years her senior. Joshua's sister Hanna was married to Silas Burke, after whom the town is named.

After becoming widowed at the age of twenty-two, Huldah Coffer began farming, growing various crops so that she could support her two daughters, Ella and Nancy, and her son, Joshua Coffer Jr.

Ella Ann Coffer was born in August 1859. She married attorney Milton Dulaney Hall, superintendent of Fairfax County Public Schools, on June 8, 1881. The couple had a daughter and a son, according to a death notice in the *Alexandria Gazette* dated October 2, 1908.

On October 1, 1908, Ella threw herself under a train and committed suicide. She told her family she was on her way to a rural delivery mailbox that afternoon and took her own life instead. She had been recently discharged from a sanitarium; what she was treated for is unknown. At first,

Coffer Cemetery circa 2023. *Author's collection.*

Woods Community Center circa 2023. *Author's collection.*

the newspapers reported that she may have misjudged the speed of the approaching train and her pace of crossing the railroad. But later, it was revealed that she lay down on the train track deliberately. It is believed that she may have been laid to rest near her parents in an unmarked grave, which was typical for suicides at the time. Her husband remarried an Elizabeth Carver on March 9, 1910, in Wake Forest, North Carolina.

Today, Ella's former home is a community center in Burke, and it seems that she hasn't left. Considering that this was the house she grew up in and lived in with not only her family but her husband as well, it's clear that the house held something special for her. Paranormal activity reports include mysterious footsteps, doors opening and closing by themselves and the overwhelming feeling of being watched.

LEE CHAPEL CEMETERY

Many drive down Lee Chapel Road in Burke, Virginia, unaware of the traumatic event that took place there over a century ago. The echoes of a young girl who was violated and killed still permeate the area, with frequent sightings continuing to this day. Not only is this one of the most disturbing cold cases in Northern Virginia, but it is also one of the most prominent ghost stories. "Help me please" and "I am Eva" forever haunt the witnesses who have seen a girl in the woods, pleading for assistance before disappearing. With this terrifying experience comes a frustrating story of gross injustice.

While the United States was approaching the last few months of World War I, fourteen-year-old Eva Roy lived in a farmhouse with her father, sister and brother-in-law in Burke's Station, Fairfax County, Virginia. The town was a tiny village that mainly relied on woodchopping and farming for its economy. Eva's father, Peter, was a Danish farmer who lived in Minnesota before relocating to Burke's Station in 1912. He was a widower and one of the most successful farmers in the area. He purchased two parcels of land totaling 180 acres. Peter was known to let his cows roam freely around the area, which often caused tension with the neighbors. Eva was popular around the village and considered beautiful and kind. She was certainly a Fairfax County favorite. Eva taught Sunday School for Lee Chapel Church, where Peter would occasionally preach.

On August 6, 1918, Peter had to go into town to tend to some business. Usually, he gathered his cows in the morning; that day, he asked young Eva to do this chore in his place. She left the house around nine o'clock with a bottle of coffee and a sack lunch. When Peter returned, he noticed that Eva hadn't come home yet, which was odd. He immediately went out to look for her. Peter found the cows but not his youngest daughter.

Concerned, Peter asked the neighbors for assistance, and they obliged. The search party worked all day and well into the night. At eight thirty the

Roy Farmhouse circa 2023. *Author's collection.*

next morning, neighbor Paul Marshall found Eva near an empty house—known as the Hanse or Haynes House—and a small spring. Eva was in a sitting position with her neck tied tightly to a tree. She was dead. A bloody trail from an open field to the wooded area showed where her body had been dragged.

Around her body were torn strips of clothing, paper from her sack lunch, broken tree branches and shoe prints. Eva was covered in scratches, teeth marks and cuts, and she had been raped.

Upon the discovery of Eva's body, county coroner Dr. Robey was called. But before Robey or any local doctors arrived at the crime scene, two women were called there to take care of Eva's body. Their well-meaning gestures included removing Eva's body to the Roy house, destroying her clothing, cutting the string around her neck and washing her body. Any evidence was completely contaminated, if not destroyed.

A coroner's jury returned a verdict of death for the murderer, even though there was no suspect yet. Basically, a jury was polled to impose a sentence before the murderer could be identified—something one would not encounter today.

Suspicion immediately fell on a man named Lou Hall, a neighbor of the Roys. He was often dirty and was known to beat his wife, Naomi Taylor Hall. Eva had recently reprimanded him for beating his wife and told him she would continue to do so if she saw it again. Hall was also irritated at Peter for allowing his cows to roam freely because the bovines would go into his garden and eat his cabbages. Hall was suspect no. 1.

Hall shared that on the morning of the murder, he went to look for honey with two other woodchoppers, but they were unsuccessful. Hall went home, ate lunch, collected his wife and daughter and took them to his in-laws' and then went to his brother's house in Accotink with his four-year old son. But Hall's in-laws said this story was strange, because he had threatened to kill Naomi if she ever set foot in her parents' home again. Naomi also said that when Hall returned home before lunch, he was "greatly excited" and all wet, like he'd gone swimming in a stream. Naomi did say that Hall told her they were leaving and dropped her and their daughter off near her parents' home. Sheriff J.R. Allison called for bloodhounds, who tracked down Hall.

Hall was not surprised when police arrested him, but that was because he thought he was being brought in for draft evasion. Hall was also freshly bathed, which was out of character, and his body was free of cuts and bruises. Meanwhile, as word spread of Eva's brutal murder, a mob gathered outside of Fairfax jail, and there was talk of lynching Hall.

However, the evidence against Hall was circumstantial. Soon, the Commonwealth of Virginia had a suspect no. 2, a Black man by the name of James Robertson, who was being held in nearby Washington, D.C., on vagrancy charges. Robertson was cleared, since there was no proof that he was in Burke's Station at the time of Eva's murder.

Suspect no. 3, a sixteen-year-old Black teen named William Wooster, was arrested but was able to prove that he was in Fairfax on the day of the murder.

Suspect no. 4 was an unnamed Black man who had escaped the nearby Lorton Reformatory the day before the murder. He was wearing his prison apron, whose strings were thought to match the apron strings found around Eva's neck. There was talk of exhuming Eva's body to check the color of the skin under her fingernails, a small detail that apparently wasn't discussed before washing, dressing and burying her body.

Suspect no. 5 was an army deserter from nearby Camp Humphries (now Fort Belvoir). When he was arrested in Charlottesville, police noticed he had scratches on his face. But Peter and his family noted that Eva bit her nails down so far that she couldn't have scratched anyone successfully. The army deserter was charged with being AWOL, but he was a drug abuser and couldn't really recount where he was the day of the murder.

Suspect no. 6 was a rumored "crazy man" who was seen by Carl Ike of Woodbridge, which was ten miles from Burke's Station. Ike claimed that the crazy man had stopped at his house and asked his two sons if they'd seen a pretty girl in the bushes who had just been murdered. The boys laughed and told him to leave. This clue led to nowhere.

News of Eva's death was reported in not only local newspapers but also almost every newspaper in Northern Virginia. Papers in Richmond, Baltimore and Washington, D.C., also covered the story. The East Coast was captivated by Eva's story.

Frustrated with the process of finding his daughter's killer, Peter ended up hiring his own private detective to help with the case. Unfortunately, the outside help that came in to assist didn't lead to new information or suspects.

Eva's body was exhumed on August 17 from its resting place at Lee Chapel Cemetery on the corner of Lee Chapel Road and Fairfax County Parkway. It was taken inside the chapel and examined by Dr. Robey and several other doctors, along with the local sheriff.

At this point, eleven days after the murder, decomposition had made it difficult to see any cuts or bruises on Eva. Pieces of her nails were taken for analysis, but the examination didn't give any additional information that would be useful for the investigation.

False evidence would also be planted under Hall's mattress. Apron strings matching the strings tied around Eva would be found, but unlike the ones from the crime scene, the strings under the mattress were not bloody. Pieces of the string were also placed next to the string found on Eva, and they were not long enough to wrap around Eva's neck.

With no viable suspects, police tried to get Hall to confess to the murder using an odd tactic. First, they placed an accomplice in the cell with him. The "prisoner" chatted with Hall and even gave him a cigarette. Several hours later, the "prisoner" jumped up and said that he saw the ghost of a young woman. Hall remained calm and said he didn't see a ghost. Apparently, that tactic must have worked in the past, if investigators were desperate enough to try it again.

Suspect no. 7 was identified on August 18 when a self-proclaimed criminologist by the name of Mr. Renfrew claimed that he saw a man on a train from Mount Vernon with cuts all over his face. As Renfrew tried to approach, the man apparently jumped off the train and ran.

Suspect no. 5, the Camp Humphries deserter, was cleared after he was taken to the murder scene and it was obvious that he had never been to the spot before. Some witnesses who claimed to see no. 5 also confirmed that this was not the same soldier they saw in Vienna, which added suspect no. 8 to the list as a completely different person. The search for suspect no. 8, the mysterious unidentified man seen in Vienna, led nowhere. Suspect no. 9 was a man named Willie Wooster, who was imprisoned at the local asylum for attacking a girl in Fairfax the same week Eva was murdered. Wooster had a solid alibi as well.

Hall was indicted for the rape and murder of Eva Roy on September 16, 1918, with a trial set for November 25 the same year.

But then suspect no. 10 came forward with a confession. His name was Ben Rubin, and after he was arrested in Washington, D.C., on September 19, 1918, he confessed to murdering Eva Roy. The twenty-one-year-old had escaped Lorton Reformatory on July 10, and he claimed he ran into Eva, asked her for food and told her he was an escaped convict. When she said she would turn him in, Rubin choked her and tied her to a tree to make it look like a suicide. When he was asked if he raped Eva, Rubin initially said no, then changed his story and said maybe.

Suspiciously, Rubin was also taken to the scene of the crime, and it was obvious he had never been there. He couldn't identify the pattern on Eva's dress, he didn't remember what she looked like—and he even leaned up against the tree where Eva was found without identifying it. When Peter

Eva Roy's grave at Lee Chapel Cemetery. *Author's collection.*

visited Rubin, he recanted his confession. It turned out that he lied because he wanted to get transferred to the Fairfax jail, which was easier to escape from. That information wouldn't be revealed until October, after Rubin successfully escaped from Fairfax and was arrested again in D.C.

The Commonwealth of Virginia stated they had new evidence to convict Hall. At this point, Hall had been in jail for four months. Unfortunately, the trial only proved how incompetent police and prosecutors really were. Forty-three witnesses testified, but much of their testimony was thrown out due to being irrelevant. It was truly a circus inside the courtroom, with no sign of justice for Eva. After deliberating for six hours, the jury voted eight for acquittal and four for conviction. The judge ordered the jurors to go back and continue deliberating, resulting in nine voting to convict Hall of second-degree murder and three voting for acquittal. Hall's case was declared a mistrial.

Hall remained in jail for four more months before he was granted a second trial. The first ballot resulted in eight for acquittal and four for conviction. The second ballot was unanimous for acquittal. Hall was a free man.

Sadly, Eva never got to see justice, and her killer was never found. Peter died almost twenty years later on January 22, 1938, and was laid to rest next to his daughter, never knowing who killed her. The story still rattles the town of what is now Burke, Virginia. Whether its citizens wish to ignore it or not, they don't have a choice, as a young girl screaming in the nearby woods by Lee Chapel Cemetery has been haunting the area for decades.

Lee Chapel no longer stands; a simple historic marker tells its story. Inside the chapel, Eva's remains were examined likely just feet, if not inches, away from where she worshiped when she was alive, praying to a God that didn't save her during her most terrifying and final moments.

As long ago as the 1970s and '80s and continuing to this day, people have reported seeing a girl in the woods, often wearing a white or blue robe or a nightgown. Often, she is heard screaming. Sometimes it's just a wail into the woods, while other times, words like, "I am Eva" and "Help me please, I am here" are heard by terrified witnesses. Sightings of Eva continue to haunt local message boards for Burke and Fairfax County. Some of the stories aren't viable, while others seem to be more truthful and genuine.

Local lore is consistent in that Eva's spirit is seen more often around her birthday, as well as Halloween. People gather annually at her resting place to pay their respects and to see if Eva will come forward.

The wooded area around Lee Chapel Cemetery and her resting place seem to be the most popular locations for sightings of Eva. She appears around dusk and shortly after dark. Her presence is often accompanied by a gust of wind and swirls of leaves. People don't realize she is a spirit until she swiftly disappears, meaning she looks just as real as the flesh on your bones. More intentional witnesses have called out to her, and it seems she answers. It is also rumored that Eva appears right before bad weather. Could it be that she is warning her community of trouble?

Eva's disturbing death is known as one of the most gruesome murders to have taken place in Fairfax County, and the legacy of her afterlife activities continues to haunt the town of Burke. Eva continues to scream for help in the woods, hoping that someday, someone will make it in time to save her. Or could it be that the trauma of Eva's death was so brutal that it was absorbed into the ground and replayed for whoever will pay attention? Either way, Eva's cries will forever continue to echo through the woods, pleading for justice that may never come.

Chantilly, Virginia

Walney Road Ghost

Right before exit 28 on Route 50 is Walney Road, which leads to the Dulles Sports Center. Today it is a paved road, but that wasn't always the case.

Walney Road is well known for a high level of car accidents, often fatal. With so much death on one road, it is unsurprising that there are ghosts left behind to tell their stories and teach others a lesson.

However, it seems that the ghost most commonly seen on Walney Road is also responsible for the road's high mortality rate. On certain nights, a ghostly hitchhiker can be seen on the road. If a driver sees him, it's strongly advised that they offer to pick him up. They have three chances to do this. If they keep driving, the hitchhiker will appear once again, farther down the road. If the driver decides to decline the hitchhiker a ride again, the specter will appear a third time. But this time, he doesn't appear on the road—he appears in the car. This usually startles the neglectful driver who ignored the hitchhiker and causes a wreck.

Where did this ghostly hitchhiker come from? Back when Walney Road was unpaved, it was common for people to walk down it. It was a safer option than nearby I-95, but it still came with its dangers. The hitchhiker's identity is unknown, and his fate remains in question. Whether he was killed or disappeared, it seems that not only is he still looking for a ride, but he will also punish those who neglect to pick him up.

Falls Church, Virginia

Even though it is included in Fairfax County, Falls Church is an independent city in the state of Virginia. It was named after an eighteenth-century parish of the Church of England, the Falls Church. Before English settlement, the area was governed by the Iroquois Confederacy, a council of several nations including the Tauxenent, Patawomeck and Matchotic peoples.

The Falls Church

The Falls Church still stands today, and the congregation continues to grow. The original building is used for recreational events. During the Civil War, it was used as a hospital for Union soldiers. The church was established as an Episcopalian church in 1732, with the initial setup and congregation put together in 1729 by William Gunnell. The brick building was constructed in 1769.

The original Falls Church today. *Author's collection.*

In terms of paranormal activity, the old church with an old cemetery in the yard—plus its history as a Civil War hospital—certainly sets the stage for a good ghost story. Over the years, residents and young thrill seekers have reported seeing people inside the original structure when there aren't any services or activity occurring. It especially causes anxiety when those who have gotten a closer look through the window see that the figures are wearing period clothing. Faces in the glass are often seen after people take photos, and the mysterious footsteps of those unseen echo through the building.

Roundtree Park

Roundtree Park sits along Annandale Road in a suburban area. From the outside, it looks like your typical park, with tennis courts, baseball fields, basketball courts, a playground, picnic tables and a hiking trail. It all looks innocent enough, and it's a central part of the community's recreational activities. There are two entrances to Roundtree Park, one off Annandale Road and the other at the end of Ted Drive, as well as the intersection of Vagabond Drive and Casilear Road.

However, behind the façade of innocence, it seems that something sinister lurks in the woods that makes itself known around dusk and well into the night. It's been called a creeper, a creature and other spooky names. This

Roundtree Park. *Author's collection.*

entity of Roundtree Park has long been the center of ghost stories, urban legends and rites of passage involving going into the park and making it out alive. It has appeared to people as a screaming voice in the woods begging for help, as well as a woman carrying her baby on a foggy night while tormenting visitors. Less fortunate people have seen a tall, dark specter with glowing red eyes that scurries and crawls out of view in an instant before chasing them out of the park. The reported activity seems to be centered on the Ted Drive entrance; the screaming voice is prevalent at the entrance on Annandale Road. Animals have been reported to act strangely as well. Rabbits have been seen frozen in place during the daytime, while nocturnal animals are brought to absolute silence when this entity is around.

So far, the identity of the screaming woman in the woods and the woman carrying her baby have yet to revealed. Could these be urban legends meant to deter mischievous teens from venturing into the park at night to partake in debauchery? Quite possibly. But there are countless stories on social media and community message boards from people who claim to have seen or interacted with the spooky activity in the park, especially the large shadow with glowing red eyes.

Most of the stories are consistent. People go to Ted Drive late at night and enter the park, just around fifty yards in. That's all they need to do to experience something off and creepy. Now, the park is closed at night, so entering late at night would technically be breaking the law.

There are houses sitting right along the entrance at Ted Drive, with windows looking into the park. One has to wonder what they see at night. Do the residents in those homes see the dark entity pacing the tree line, staying away from the light? Do dark spirits look into these homes?

HARPER HOUSE

Harper House started off as a barn for George Mason in the Greenway Downs neighborhood. The historic house in Falls Church with over two hundred years of history burned down in January 1976 due to faulty wiring. It was a massive loss, as it was not only a house linked to George Mason, but George Washington's horse also slept in the barn. Washington would often visit Mason after attending the Falls Church. Washington and Mason would enjoy a cup of cider under the tree on Sunday afternoons while Washington's horse slept in the barn.

In 1934, a man by the name of Carl Harper purchased the barn and converted it into a house. Harper had quite the legacy of his own: he taught Amelia Earhart how to fly a plane. But one thing Carl lacked was general knowledge of how to build a house. This resulted in the house going through a unique remodeling job, and it was poorly put together.

Eventually, the house became known as the "spook house." The couple that owned the house when it burned down, Ronald and Dominique Hodge, lived there with Mrs. Hodge's sons from a previous marriage, Jody and Shaun. It seems that Dominique and Jody encountered paranormal activity numerous times during their residency. Neighbors also reported strangeness surrounding the house. One of the more notable sightings was the apparitions of Carl Harper and his wife.

In an interview with the *Globe*, Dominique Hodge said she was standing on the first floor with a friend one day when she looked up to the gallery—which was once a hayloft and now a bedroom area—and saw a short man with white hair and a deeply lined face. As she and her friend looked up, the man stepped back into the shadows. Her friend was terrified and left the house immediately.

Lorton, Virginia

Pohick Church

The congregation itself dates to the 1720s. The original site of the church was about two miles south, where the modern-day Cranford United Methodist Church now stands. It was later renamed Pohick Church due to how close it is to the Pohick River. The present-day Pohick Church was commissioned in 1767, and the building opened its doors in 1774 as Occoquan Church.

This building saw many turbulent times, and the fact that it is still standing is nothing short of a miracle. It was considered the "Mother Church" of Northern Virginia, and it was the first church built north of the Occoquan River. The land was surveyed by George Washington himself. Washington was one of the church's most dedicated members and rarely missed a Sunday. The church is also associated with two other famous men named George, George Mason and George Fairfax, earning it the nickname Church of the Three Georges. It started off as an Anglican church, but by the War of 1812, it had become an Episcopalian church.

Top: Historic photo of Pohick Church. *Library of Congress.*

Bottom: Pohick Church circa 2023. *Author's collection.*

During the War of 1812, the British acknowledged the importance of the church and proceeded to deface it. In fact, they even beheaded a statue of a golden dove that sat on Washington's pew. The headless dove was found in the courtyard and passed through a few generations of owners before it was returned to the church in 1988.

After the War of 1812, Pohick Church was abandoned until about 1837. An Episcopalian bishop visited Pohick Church and was horrified to see the condition it was in. He proceeded to raise about $1,500 for repairs, with contributions from Francis Scott Key, former president John Quincy Adams, Henry Clay, Daniel Webster and President Martin Van Buren.

As fate would have it, just as Pohick Church was ready to reopen, the Civil War started. The Union army raided the church and used it as a stable for its horses. After the war ended, the church reopened in 1878. But once again, it needed to be restored. The Mount Vernon Ladies Association and the Mount Vernon chapter of the Daughters of the American Revolution raised funds to bring the church back to its former glory. Today, the church is still functioning, with regular services.

There are a few rumors of ghosts around the Pohick Church. Considering it saw so much war in its lifetime and nearly didn't survive, it would not be a shock if a few souls were still hanging about. However, the urban legend and ghost lore surrounds an eccentric millionaire and a tomb that went unused...

THE REMEUM

The Remey family mausoleum, also known as the Remeum, was positioned behind Pohick Church. It was built by famous architect, lecturer and author Charles Mason Remey. Remey had his share of tragedy in his life. He was married to Gertrude Heim Klemm from July 17, 1931, until her suicide by two bullets on August 5, 1932.

The Remeum cost about $1 million, making it one of the most expensive projects in Northern Virginia at the time. The tomb was designed to look like a temple of the Bahá'í faith. Construction started in 1939, and Remey had previously buried family members reinterred in the Remeum.

Remey's lifelong dreams of building a massive mausoleum were inspired by a visit to a burial vault on his grandfather's farm in Iowa. When he was just eight years old, Remey gathered bricks and stones to build a tomb in his garden at home.

In a quest to build his own massive family vault, Remey purchased five acres of land behind Pohick Church. It also took about two million bricks to build the Remeum, which included marble vaults and was designed to be a family crypt for the Remey family. It was technically never completed, and by the 1950s, it had become a focal point of urban legends by locals and the youth. People were curious about what was inside the crypt and started breaking into the tomb. In 1956, a group of teenagers was fined after punching a hole through a brick wall to get in. The statues of Remey's family members were vandalized, with many beheaded. From there, people started reporting strange things happening at the tomb, such as ill feelings around it, the feeling of being watched and shadows wandering in the woods and around the mausoleum.

A legal battle was fought between the Remey family and the Northern Virginia government over the land and how it was being used. By the 1960s, Remey had relocated to Italy, and Pohick Church was tired of the constant vandalism. Because the tomb didn't have a foreseeable completion date, and it would continue to be an eyesore, Remey was forced to give the land back to the local government, which resulted in church leaders having to take care of the property. The responsibility of dealing with the structure was given to Pohick Church and its leaders, and the church decided to start dismantling the structure. The walls were torn down, which opened up opportunities for teens to break into the crypt. They started having parties in the mausoleum, resulting in more vandalism

Church leaders realized they were liable for injuries in the crypt. So in 1983, they decided to cover the entire tomb with cement so no one could get in—which only intensified speculation around the urban legend. The vandalized statues were further buried in the depths of the mausoleum. All that's left of the structure is the obelisk with two chimney vents.

Colchester Inn, just a few miles from Pohick Church. *Library of Congress.*

Charles Remey had beautiful statues of his deceased family created and placed in the tomb, which were vandalized in the '60s and '70s. The bodies that were present were removed from the crypt.

The church got rid of majority of the structure and planted trees to cover the footprint of the tomb. However, people still visit the area and try to get in. Legend has it that there may be hidden treasure or that there are multiple floors within the tomb, prompting urban explorers to check it out. Visitors looking for the sealed entrance late at night have reported feelings of being watched and a heaviness in the air.

Legends and lore about spiritual caretakers often surround cemeteries and tombs. Even though the Remeum was never officially completed, perhaps a guardian was waiting to take care of the place? Or perhaps Remey and his family watch over the area, since they basically had the land taken from them and their final resting place—at least the one they wanted—was never completed. All Remey really wanted was to ensure that his family legacy was permanently marked in the history books. It seems there is a presence ensuring that this happens.

THE JAMMES HOUSE

The 1,800-acre Mason Neck State Park is a popular spot for recreational activities like fishing, hiking, birdwatching, biking and more. Its forest terrain offers plenty of trees for shade, and wetlands, ponds and open fields give recreationists abundant ways to enjoy the outdoors.

Mason Neck is named for the Mason family, which includes George Mason. The Neck was the name of the surrounding land that was home to the Masons. A housewife by the name of Liz Hartwell actively worked to preserve the land within the Neck, and it's thanks to her that people can enjoy it today.

One house that has been preserved and sits on the property today is the Jammes House. The house was once occupied by a man known as Dr. Juan L. Jammes, a neurologist from Argentina; his wife, Francine; and their two daughters. The two-story house stands about twenty feet above the Occoquan Bay.

In March 1994, Dr. Jammes and Francine went to Yellowstone National Park to go on holiday. On March 24, Francine was driving a snowmobile and her husband was riding with her when they hit a tree. They were declared dead on the scene. Dr. Jammes was only fifty-five years old,

Francine just fifty-one. According to a March 30, 1994 article in the *Jackson Hole News*, their teenage daughters were on another snowmobile at the time of the accident.

The Department of Recreation and Conservation purchased the Jammes House after the estate was settled and started using the home as a hunting lodge, for overnight accommodations for staff and volunteers and as a meetinghouse for public events.

In the book *Ghostly Tales of Selected Virginia State Parks*, author P.M. Elton retells the paranormal experiences that have occurred in the Jammes House. According to Elton, visitors have reported feeling uneasy when they enter the house. The house is also cold on a constant basis, no matter what the temperature is outside. The house also has many empty rooms and bathrooms, which brings about feelings of uneasiness in visitors. There are reports of people walking through the house when no one is present. The top of the stairs is said to be haunted by the spirit of a young girl. A door to the left of the staircase opens onto a wall. A tiny pink bathroom on the second floor disturbs visitors so much that they won't go in there because it's believed a ghost is behind the shower curtain, waiting to scare the next visitor.

Elton also retells the story of the park's executive director and her adventure spending the night in one of the house's most haunted rooms. As she attempted to sleep, she kept hearing a swooshing sound and feeling something rushing back and forth across the room. She got through the night by pulling the covers up over her head as much as possible.

In the first-floor master bedroom, there is a painting of one of the Jammes daughters. But she is not the little girl who haunts the second story.

It seems that the house itself is not haunted by any members of the Jammes family, which is a good thing. But that only leaves another thread of mystery: who remains? Perhaps it is a transient spirit looking for a new place to call home? An old house overlooking the Occoquan Bay and the Potomac River is a fine choice, indeed.

LAZY SUSAN DINNER THEATRE

The Lazy Susan Dinner Theatre is no longer functioning, as it closed in October 2013, and it looks like the original building has been torn down. Today, there is a Pentecostal church in its place in a very large, industrial-size building.

But in Lazy Susan's heyday, it was very much a hub where the community of Lorton could take in a play or a musical while enjoying a meal. As Lorton is quite the historic town with a loaded history—plus, with the common trope of all theaters having a ghost, it's almost expected that there would have been a ghost or two.

There was a ghost at the Lazy Susan Dinner Theatre who reportedly enjoyed making appearances onstage in the form of gliding lights, as well as rearranging tables and chairs. Perhaps this spirit was a thespian in life and was looking for another go-round onstage in the afterlife.

OCCOQUAN WORKHOUSE

The Occoquan Workhouse's history is devastating, sordid and a testament to what revitalization can do for a community. At the turn of the twentieth century, prisons were known for overcrowding, deplorable conditions and horrific abuse. The Occoquan Workhouse, also known as the Lorton Workhouse, was built in 1910 as an industrial farm. This type of prison was an experiment to test the effectiveness of hard labor as a form of rehabilitation for medium-security prisoners. This workhouse was literally built by the prisoners themselves. Bricks were made on-site, and prisoners constructed their future home.

In 1912, a women's workhouse opened nearby, whose inmates had mainly been found guilty of prostitution, drunkenness and disorderly conduct. Women were placed in the laundry room, among other work areas, to serve out their sentences.

On November 14 and 15, 1917, the women's workhouse got a very different and rather unique set of prisoners: the Silent Sentinels. This group of women was fighting for women's right to vote and protesting in Washington, D.C. The group was part of the National Woman's Party, led by Alice Paul and Lucy Burns.

Sadly, the Silent Sentinels were subjected to horrific abuse and torture at the hands of about forty prison guards. They were beaten and chained, and their heads were bashed into iron bedframes. An elderly suffragette was even stabbed with the wooden pole of her own picket sign. Lucy Burns was handcuffed with her arms above her head and forced to stay that way all night. The next day, she was stripped and placed outside in the freezing cold.

When their treatment made the mainstream news, it was seen as all the more shocking because these women were part of high society, had a certain

Workhouse Arts Center circa 2023. *Author's collection.*

social status and were seen as respectable. The group was subjected to beds riddled with bugs, and their food was not much better. Alice Paul attempted a hunger strike to protest the poor treatment of the women in the prison, but she was soon force-fed raw eggs. This wouldn't be her only hunger strike while in the prison. But instead of these feeling discouraged and stopping their fight for equal rights, these women were more inspired than ever. When the public found out just how poorly they were treated, they too joined the cause. The Nineteenth Amendment was eventually passed in 1919, giving women the right to vote.

Other prisoners weren't subjected to such awful conditions during their time at the workhouse, which spotlights how this political cause fueled horrific treatment. Other prisoners were able to enjoy recreational activities. In the 1960s, celebrities like Ella Fitzgerald and Frank Sinatra visited and performed at the prison. The prison was eventually shut down in 2001, and inmates were transferred to other facilities.

After the closure, the workhouse began to decay. Urban explorers found ways inside the prison. Visitors have reported hearing voices on the grounds and seeing the shadows of unidentifiable people. They've also felt they were being watched, an intense heaviness and a certain level of anxiety. Given the abuse and trauma perpetuated at the workhouse, it could certainly hold residual energy from that time.

The building was transformed into the Workhouse Art Center in 2008, with galleries, art studios, a theater and other spaces dedicated to community engagement and education. The Workhouse Prison Museum features the Silent Sentinels and is dedicated to telling their story. The space has gone through its share of healing as the community takes over. But will that be enough to satisfy the spirits that remain?

GUNSTON HALL

George Mason was one of the Founding Fathers of the United States, and he wrote the Virginia Declaration of Rights, which would become the foundation for the U.S. Bill of Rights. George Mason University was named after him and is one of the largest academic institutions in Northern Virginia.

In 1754, George had inherited an old house, but he and his wife, Ann, wanted a more modern one. Construction of Gunston Hall started that same year and was completed four years later. The house was designed based on the latest architectural trends in England, and it was incredibly spacious. The bricks were made by enslaved people, and the exterior was built by a mason, assisted by the enslaved. George's brother Thomson managed to find a skilled craftsman, a young man by the name of William Buckland, to design and build the interior of the house. Buckland agreed to an indentured contract of four years, and he was assisted by another indentured servant by the name of William Bernard Sears.

Gunston Hall circa 2023. *Author's collection.*

George lived at his estate, Gunston Hall, for the rest of his life. It seems that George loved his home so much that he doesn't want to leave. His apparition has been spotted in mirrors. Other reports include unexplained footsteps in the hall and sightings of apparitions wearing eighteenth-century clothing both inside and outside the house.

But George isn't the only apparition that has been seen at Gunston Hall. Other entities have been seen throughout the property, who could be members of his family or other visitors who have helped maintain the property over the years. Employees at Gunston Hall wear costumes, and it's believed that this action triggers the paranormal events.

ANNANDALE, VIRGINIA

OAK HILL MANSION

Oak Hill Mansion in Annandale, Virginia, was built around 1790 by Richard Fitzhugh on twenty-two thousand acres of the Ravensworth Tract, one of the largest land grants given in the New World. Richard and his wife, Suzanna, would go on to have eight children while living there. Today, Oak Hill Mansion is privately owned after being saved by land developers. Part of the agreement with the Fairfax County Board of Supervisors and historic preservation activists was that the owners must open the house up to the public once a year.

Oak Hill is also known as Miss Ann's Mansion. Legend says that Miss Ann Fitzhugh died protecting her English love, Captain Charles Hawkins. Ann Fitzhugh accompanied her father, Richard, to England on business. While she was there, she fell in love with Charles. When rumblings of the Revolutionary War began, the Fitzhughs returned to Virginia, but Ann and Charles kept in touch. Charles was sent to Virginia to stop the colonial rebellion, and he visited Ann several times at Oak Hill.

When Federal troops learned that an English captain was visiting Oak Hill, they surrounded the house. Ann and Charles hid in a secret room above the dining room, which was accessible by a trapdoor. Realizing no one was around, the Federal troops were starting to leave—when a soldier poked either a saber or a bayonet through the trapdoor. Unfortunately, Ann was above the trapdoor and was stabbed, killing her. Charles jumped through a window in the attic and managed to escape. Ann's spirit is said to remain at Oak Hill, crying and pleading for Charles to return to her.

Oak Hill Mansion. *Jerrye & Roy Klotz, MD.*

This story first emerged in 1941 when the Fairfax Garden Club did tours at Oak Hill, and then it reemerged in 1961 in the *Historical Society of Fairfax Yearbook* by Mrs. Edward F. Howrey. Mrs. Howrey owned Oak Hill with her husband from 1935 until 1968.

It seems, though, that the story is more fiction than anything else. Oak Hill didn't exist during the Revolutionary War, since it was built in 1793. There really was an Ann Fitzhugh who lived at Oak Hill, but she married a man named Charles R. Battalie, Esq., and they lived in Culpeper, Virginia. There really was a Captain Charles Hawkins, but he was an officer in the Alexandria Sharp-Shooters in 1842. It's not certain that he knew Ann.

But that doesn't discount the idea that there could be some sort of paranormal activity occurring at Oak Hill. We just know that it likely isn't Ann reliving those events. It's said that she cries out to Charles; it could very well be her own husband she is pining for in the afterlife.

ANNANDALE HIGH SCHOOL

The boys' restroom at Annandale High School is reported to be home to the spirit of a boy who died by suicide. The apparition of the young man is often spotted in the bathroom mirrors.

Clifton, Virginia

Bunny Man Bridge

I would be remiss—if not committing a crime—not to bring up the legend of the Bunny Man. As I was doing research for the book, people kept saying, "Have you heard of Bunny Man Bridge?" or "Make sure you include the Bunny Man!" Certainly, the story of the Bunny Man and the bridge is probably the most famous legend of the area, mentioned in numerous books as well as news segments every Halloween season.

Who is the Bunny Man? Where did the legend come from? Where is the actual Bunny Man Bridge? Is the Bunny Man a ghost or cryptid? These are all questions I was asking myself as I talked to people about the legend.

The stories about the Bunny Man vary depending on who you talk to and what region they're from. Extensive research has been done to determine whether the Bunny Man was a real person, perhaps a serial killer from an earlier time who became so notorious that his story outlived him.

The earliest account of the Bunny Man goes back to 1970, when two incidents took place in Fairfax County. By 1973, the legend had extended to Washington, D.C., and Maryland. The infamous Bunny Man Bridge is the Colchester Overpass, a Southern Railway overpass that goes over Colchester Road in Clifton.

According to local historian Brian A. Conley, in 1970, on Guinea Road in Burke, Virginia, there were two incidents in which a man in a rabbit costume threatened people with an axe. The first incident happened on October 19, when U.S. Air Force Academy cadet Robert Bennett and his fiancée were visiting relatives in the area. They parked their car in a field across the street from an uncle they were visiting. The couple was in the car, which was still running, when the front window was smashed. A figure dressed in white stood next to the broken window, screaming at the couple that they were trespassing and he had their tag number. Robert turned the car around and drove away. As they were getting away, the couple noticed there was a hatchet on the floor of the car. They went to the police, and when Robert claimed that the man was dressed in a white suit with bunny ears, his fiancée corrected him, saying that the man was dressed in a white hood. They both saw his face but couldn't determine his race.

The second reported sighting happened ten days later, on October 29, when a construction security guard named Paul Phillips approached a man standing on the porch of a home that was being built. The man was dressed in a bunny costume and was chopping at the porch with an axe, proclaiming that Phillips was trespassing and if he got any closer, he would chop off his head.

During this time, there were over fifty additional reports of a man in a bunny costume in the area. But due to lack of evidence, police couldn't pursue a case, and so they dropped it. The local newspapers started running stories on the Bunny Man sightings, inciting panic in the community.

It didn't take long for a story to come out claiming that the Bunny Man was a convict who escaped prison in 1904 while being transported to a new facility and his name was Douglas J. Griffon. Another variation of the story says Griffon was a mental asylum patient in Clifton. Because the residents of Clifton didn't want the facility in their town, all the patients were transported to an asylum in Lorton. During the trip, the bus swerved and crashed. All but one patient was found, and the missing patient was Griffon. After that, rabbit skins and corpses started appearing in the woods, as Griffon was eating rabbits to stay alive. From there, a series of grisly and supernatural murders occurred in the area. However, there is no historical documentation to support that these events happened. Additionally, the locations noted in the legend did not exist at the time.

Ever since, stories of the Bunny Man and the bridge have been cultivated, and the character has evolved into an axe-wielding maniac who skins rabbits—or, more gruesomely, skins teenagers and other curious visitors. One of the riskiest things you can do is hang out around Bunny Man Bridge on Halloween night, because you could meet a violent demise. One could call the Bunny Man legend a modern Grimm's fairy tale that teaches kids and teenagers a lesson about staying out late at night.

How could Bunny Man Bridge be haunted by someone who likely never existed? There are theories that our conscious minds can communicate with ghosts through sheer will. In the 1970s, a group of parapsychologists in Toronto, Canada, met on a weekly basis to test the power of manifestation by creating their own spirit named Philip in what they called the Philip Experiment. The mainstream paranormal community calls this phenomenon a thoughtform or a tulpa, a phenomenon connected to Tibetan Buddhism whereby one creates their own entity with their mind.

Is it possible that the Bunny Man is indeed a real entity now because so many people have come together to tell the story? Perhaps the only spirit of the Bunny Man that exists is the one that has been created by mass collective consciousness and intention—which may be even more terrifying than an actual ghost.

MOUNT VERNON, VIRGINIA

MOUNT VERNON

Mount Vernon, located in Fairfax County, is famous as the homestead of George Washington. It started off as a one-story building built by Augustine Washington, George's father, in 1734. The house got its famous name from George's brother Lawrence. George inherited Mount Vernon in 1754 and he spent the next forty-five years growing the one-story house into the massive mansion it eventually became. George had a hand in every expansion and renovation, while conscious that all eyes were on him as the first president of the United States as well as a gentleman of Virginia. What is incredible to consider is that Mount Vernon is ten times larger than the average colonial home of the time.

In December 1799, George fell ill, and he ended up passing away at Mount Vernon. This could be why George's spirit is so active around Mount Vernon. Not only was he incredibly involved in expanding the home, but he also passed away in his beloved mansion.

Ghost stories associated with the plantation home date as far back as the 1890s, when members of the Mount Vernon Ladies Association reported having paranormal experiences in Washington's bedroom. Two members spent the night there, and Washington's figure appeared hovering over the women as they slept in bed, positioned the same way it was the night he passed away.

In the 1980s, a historical interpreter reported seeing the full-bodied apparition of a young woman carrying flowers down the stairs. By the time she reached the bottom, she had completely disappeared.

In 2012, a security guard who was locking up the house at night reported hearing a set of keys jingling in Washington's bedroom. In life, George Washington was known to carry a heavy set of keys, which would jingle as he walked.

There's another interesting phenomenon at Mount Vernon, though: a potential cryptid. In 1979, Blaine Harden wrote an article for the *Washington Post* about the Mount Vernon Monster screaming in the night. Witnesses have said that the sound the creature makes is deep and loud enough to rattle windows and it moved quickly from one end of the house to the other. One witness named Thelma Crisp, who lived nearby, said that she spotted the creature and described it as being around six feet tall, walking upright. However, naysayers claim that the sound from 1979 was from kids putting speakers in their window. Could Mount Vernon be home to its own Bigfoot? Considering that sightings have been few and far between, it's possible that this is a hoax—or the creature got better at hiding.

HERNDON, VIRGINIA

Herndon, Virginia, is a little over twenty-four miles west of Washington, D.C., and close to Dulles airport. In 1917, the small town experienced a catastrophic fire that caused significant damage.

DEAD MAN'S HOLLOW

Herndon has its own Dead Man's Hollow alongside Arlington. Herndon's Dead Man's Hollow is near a small, winding creek on a lonely road. The story comes from Frances Darlington Simpson Onacewicz, daughter of a prominent Washington lawyer named Joseph J. Darlington. He inherited a grand summer home from his grandfather in the town of Herndon and lived there from around 1890 until his passing in 1920. Onacewicz wrote a cookbook titled *Virginia Country Life and Cooking*, and in it, she retold a ghost story she often heard in her youth.

Onacewicz writes,

> *Herndon is not without its ghost. Several years after my grandfather bought the Herndon place, a man was brutally murdered close to a small winding creek between Herndon and the Leesburg Pike.*
>
> *This is not just another murder, it seems, unsolved and forgotten, for people crossing the creek reported a hideous feeling of being pursued and touched by the cold, clammy hand of DEATH.*
>
> *These reports continued over the years until finally the creek became known as Dead Man's Hollow. Nobody seems to know who the murdered man was or exactly how he met his dreadful fate but every time one passes over the bridge, one briefly but invariably feels through the mist something reaching and clutching, a momentary but spine-chilling encounter with the DEAD. It is said that the restless spirit of the dead man searches and searches for his murderer.*

In a brief but blood curdling experience...my youngest son tells me with great conviction that even on a hot summer's day at noon, whenever he and his friends hurry past Dead Man's Hollow, they too feel a paralyzing chill as the restless Ghost reaches for his murderer with the icy fingers of the DEAD!

The location of Dead Man's Hollow remains in question.

BRUSH STROKES

In an article dated October 4, 2017, on the website Patch, author Barbara Glakas writes about a ghost story surrounding a hair salon called Brush Strokes. The house where Brush Strokes resides was built around 1900, if not earlier, on 711 Pine Street. The property itself was owned by former mayor Elisha Dyer in the late 1800s. In 1888, a dentist named Dr. Ben Detwiler purchased the property from Dyer. About five years later, Dr. Ben sold it to his brother, Dr. Edwin Detwiler. It seems that both brothers ran their practices out of that house.

Sadly, in 1916, the son of a patient tracked down Dr. Ed while he was on a house call and shot the doctor dead. After that, the house was sold to the Wheeler family, who lived there for many years. From there, it was sold to Dr. Finley's Family Eyecare business; he later moved the business to another building on the same street.

In 1998, Mary E. Taylor bought the building and turned it into Brush Strokes. She wanted to create a cozy feeling, so she decorated it with soothing colors, antique furniture and lace curtains. More notably, she displayed a photo of Dr. Edwin Detwiler in the foyer.

Taylor then held an open house to welcome the public to her new salon. One of the attendees was an elderly woman by the name of Roberta "Bobby" Keys. It turns out that Keys was the grandniece of Dr. Ed and the granddaughter of Dr. Ben. Keys told Taylor how she would often play in her uncle's office. She also said to Taylor, "I love what you've done to the place." Keys passed away a short time later.

One client came in to have her hair cut, with her twenty-year-old daughter along for the appointment. The daughter was known to be sensitive. As she sat in the foyer, she started to feel some strange energy. She then saw a little girl sitting on the foyer floor. The little girl said to her, "I love what you've done to the place." Could it be that Mrs. Keys returned to her uncle's home that she loved so much?

Other reported paranormal activity includes a strange energy, but it's a positive presence. That's a good thing for Taylor, indeed.

THE GRIFFIN-OWENS INSURANCE AGENCY

Barbara Glakas also wrote about another haunted location in Herndon: the Griffin-Owens Insurance Company. The building started off as a home and was built around the 1920s. During the 1940s and '50s, the home was occupied by a couple named George and Agnes Chappell. After George passed away in 1959, Agnes continued to live in the house, and she rented out the other rooms until her death in 1981.

In 1982, a man named Joe Skaggs bought the house and converted it into an office for his construction company. In 1989, he built an extension to the house. That same year, Skaggs had reported to the *Reston Times* that he and his staff were experiencing unusual activity, such as strange noises and weird sightings in the building. It is not uncommon for renovations and construction to stir up paranormal activity.

One night, three of Skaggs's friends camped out inside the house. One of them woke up to see an elderly lady standing at the foot of his sleeping bag. Another friend woke up, and he, too, saw the elderly lady over by his friend. The trio had asked Skaggs if anyone else would be staying in the house that night, and he said no.

On a different night, Skaggs's secretary and her sister were sleeping in the attic when they heard footsteps on the stairs. Frightened, the secretary called 911, only for law enforcement to find that no one was there. Skaggs also mentioned that he couldn't keep nighttime custodians employed, as they would often quit soon after starting.

Initially, Skaggs didn't believe in the ghost stories. But he became a believer after he saw a ghost for himself. He, too, saw the elderly lady standing at the kitchen door. He described her as looking like a grandmother with stooped shoulders.

In 2003, the Griffin-Owens Insurance Agency purchased the building. In 2016, several of the insurance company's employees came forward to share their own stories of paranormal experiences. One employee said that she heard footsteps above her one night, as if they were coming from the attic. Another employee said, "Sometimes I can feel her."

A third employee came forward and shared an experience she had one night while working late. It was a busy time, and phone calls were constantly coming in. Looking down the hallway, she saw a woman in white clothing. When the employee asked the woman in white to come over so she could help her, the woman went into the fax room. The employee followed her into the fax room and realized that no one was there. She went to another employee to ask if they had gone into the fax room, intending to identify the woman in the white, but she realized that her coworker was wearing red, so it couldn't have been her.

The employee quickly accepted that she had seen a ghost. She described the woman in white as an elderly lady with stooped shoulders and blonde hair with streaks of grey. This employee was not familiar with the 1989 *Reston Times* article in which Joe Skaggs described the same woman.

Glakas did some detective work and found one of George and Agnes Chappell's nieces. When Glakas described the woman to the niece, the niece said she was certain it wasn't her aunt, as her aunt was big-boned with broad shoulders and brown hair. However, the niece mentioned that the elderly woman might be her grandmother Lutie, as she often visited the house. Glakas got a photo of Lutie and showed it to the employee who had seen the woman in white. The employee confirmed that the woman in the photo looked very much like the woman she saw that night. Even though Lutie didn't live on the property, she often came to visit Agnes. It seems that she developed an affection for the property, since she either resides in the building as a ghost or visits often.

George Mason University

GEORGE MASON UNIVERSITY POND

The pond at George Mason University is reportedly haunted by a young man who drowned in the nearby lake. Two women found his body sitting in the gazebo the next morning. Legend has it that the young man has often been seen standing at the edge of the lake or sitting under the gazebo, which doesn't actually exist today. He will ask young women to sit with him under "the gazebo." As soon as he's approached, he disappears.

To learn more about this entity and his presence at Mason, I interviewed Ang DiNardo, president of Mason's Folklore Roundtable. DiNardo—who first heard about this ghost as a freshman back in 2004—isn't sure how the legend started, but it's been around for a long time. (One of DiNardo's former professors graduated from GMU in the mid-to-late '90s, and they knew the story from their time as a student.) There are actually two variants of the story, but the common thread is that there was a young man who drowned in the Mason Pond. Some speculate that it was a suicide after he

Top: George Mason University Pond. *Author's collection.*

Bottom: George Mason University Fenwick Library. *Author's collection.*

was stood up on a date, in the vein of the "jilted lover" trope. However, the GMU Police Department claims that there have been no deaths related to the pond.

Along the wooded path that goes past the pond, there's a little house. DiNardo isn't sure what it's used for—perhaps storage or water pumps. When a young woman is walking down that path, the ghost of the young man will appear to her. He will try to take her hand and pull her into the water. DiNardo told me that there are people on campus who claim they know someone who has had an encounter with the Pond Ghost, also known as the Gazebo Ghost (even though there is no longer a gazebo). DiNardo speculates that perhaps there was a gazebo where the house is today, but it's difficult to know for sure.

Another building on campus also has its own ghost story. A staff member disclosed to DiNardo that they've experienced something unexplainable inside. Details cannot be shared at this time due to permissions and privacy concerns, but this story goes to show that while Mason Pond is the star of the local ghost stories, there could be other ghosts lingering around campus.

DiNardo told me that this staff member also encountered the ghost of Eva Roy back in 2023. At the time, the legend about her was unknown to them.

Certainly, just because a building is new, that doesn't necessarily mean it isn't haunted. If ghostly activity is occurring, it could be due to something attached to the land or even a spirit that passed by and found the building an appealing place to reside in.

OLD MAN JOHNSON

Another story that haunts the students of Mason was collected by a member of Mason's Folklore Roundtable back in 2003, but DiNardo notes that the story has likely been around much longer. During that time, the English Department was collecting local stories and legends. This roundtable member found the story of Old Man Johnson and realized that it was connected to the women's crew team.

I asked DiNardo to tell me the legend of Old Man Johnson. He used to linger around the area in the 1970s. Johnson came home one day and found his wife in bed with another man. He was so upset that he went out to row—and he never came back. Some people say he rowed over the dam, while others say he jumped off.

The women's rowing team has reported seeing Johnson's ghost during their early morning practices, near either the docks or the dam. Anytime the team encounters anything strange, they blame it on Old Man Johnson. I asked DiNardo if the men's crew team had experienced this too. DiNardo wasn't sure—but knew for certain that Old Man Johnson is associated with the women's team.

A RITE OF PASSAGE

As DiNardo and I closed out our conversation, it became evident that the lore around George Mason University has a much deeper meaning than just a few ghost stories. DiNardo compares sharing ghost stories to a rite of passage, so to speak—meaning that when you're standing in front of the statue of George Mason and people start sharing these stories with you, it truly makes you feel like you're part of the community.

CHAPTER 9
FAUQUIER COUNTY

Putting Fauquier County in a book about Northern Virginia was a risk I was willing to take. If you ask residents of the area, they will tell you that Fauquier is not part of NOVA but instead the Piedmont part of the state. They're not wrong. But on the other hand, several maps include Fauquier County as part of Northern Virginia. Considering that the county is less than an hour away from Arlington and about half an hour away from Manassas, one could argue that it is close enough.

Fauquier County was established from Prince William County in 1759. Like several of the other locations in this book, it was first scouted out by Captain John Smith, who reported that the land was occupied by the Manahoac tribe. They were driven out by the Iroquois around 1670 and didn't return. The Conoy people camped near the town called the Plains from 1697 to 1699. In 1722, in the Treaty of Albany, the Six Nations ceded the entire region to the Virginia Colony. Several Civil War battles were fought at Fauquier, leaving their share of trauma and folklore. This means that Fauquier County has a few haunted locations that are certainly accessible to anyone in Northern Virginia and visiting tourists—and are well worth the time.

Warrenton, Virginia

The Fauquier History Museum at the Old Jail

This jail has seen its share of incredible U.S. history. The United States was less than fifty years old, and Founding Fathers like Thomas Jefferson was still alive when it was built. The Old Jail saw the Civil War, Reconstruction, Prohibition, the woman suffrage movement, World War I and World War II and the civil rights movement. The jail saw prisoners from every era who were incarcerated for various reasons, from criminal activity to defending their country and fighting for their rights.

The Old Jail in Warrenton was built in two parts. The front part of the jail was built in 1808 and had four cells. According to historical records, each cell was able to hold about forty prisoners, which seems a bit dense given the size of the building. Conditions were poor for the prisoners, with occasional visits from the jailer, meaning the prisoners were not well supervised, let alone well taken care of. Prisoners broke windows, fought with each other and tried to escape. The jail was also filthy, and prisoners made desperate attempts to get out. It was so bad that the Commonwealth of Virginia sued the jailer in 1818 over the jail's deplorable conditions.

About fifteen years after the original jail was built, in 1823, a new one was built to the rear of the old structure, as the 1808 jail was deemed to be inefficient. The inefficient jail was then converted into a house for the jailer (so hopefully they could make more regular rounds). In 1824, a kitchen was added from the leftover building supplies for the 1823 building. The Town of Warrenton also added a whipping post, stocks and a pillory in front of the 1808 building. There was an exercise yard behind the new building, which had four cells. But this time, each cell had a stove, which would keep prisoners warm. Behind the 1823 building, there was an exercise yard that doubled as an execution area, including a gallows.

In 1964, the Town of Warrenton started building a new jail, and so the two historic buildings from 1808 and 1823 were put on the list for demolition. Thankfully, the people of Fauquier County saw their historical value and created the Fauquier Historical Society with the intent of turning the 1808 and 1823 buildings into a museum and preserving the jail.

The 1808 building is used as the museum entrance, with a war room, hallway and kitchen on the first floor. The second floor includes the director's office, a research room, storage areas, a dental exhibit and a Virginia room. Behind the building is the courtyard and the 1823 building, with an industry room and an 1823 jail cell on the first floor. The second floor of the 1823 building holds maximum security cells as well as the Harway room. Behind the 1823 building is the exercise and execution area.

As the two buildings have witnessed so much historical action, it's unsurprising that there may be a few prisoners and their family members sticking around. Former director of the Old Jail Museum Frances R. Allshouse received enough reports of paranormal experiences at the location to write a book called *Ghosts of the Old Jail* with her husband and illustrator, Andrew B. Allshouse, in 2013. In the book, she reviews twenty relevant experiences ranging from guests to staff that worked at the Old Jail.

Common activity includes the sound of footsteps on the second floor as well as something dragging across the floor. The presence of children has also been noted. Not every person who was at the jail was a criminal, and sometimes people would voluntarily enlist themselves to live there, often taking their families with them because they had no other means to take care of their loved ones.

The maximum-security cell has its share of activity, especially for women. Allshouse's book includes the story of two British women who were visiting the maximum-security cell and felt someone grabbing their wrist and elbow and escorting them out.

Staff members have felt the overwhelming sensation of being watched. More disturbingly, some have felt flat-out unwelcome when working after hours, to the point where they will leave their work as it stands and get back to it in the morning. Animals have also had reactions to the jail, especially the kitchen, which was the site of a significant event: a jailer's wife burning alive while cooking a meal for the inmates. While there's no evidence that the animals are detecting that moment in history, it's notable that they've had reactions to that spot. Several paranormal investigators have visited the Old Jail to validate the reports of paranormal activity.

BLACK HORSE MANOR

Also known as the Black Horse Inn, this bed-and-breakfast earned its name from the Black Horse Calvary, a Confederate unit that beat the Union during the First Battle of Manassas. It is believed that the house was built around the 1850s and served as a hospital during the Civil War.

Additions to the home were made in the twentieth century. The Black Horse Manor as it exists today has ten rooms, each with its own private bathroom. The manor today has paid special attention to making sure that the interior remains historic.

Reports of the paranormal at the manor include activity from at least four different ghosts. A laughing nurse has been sighted, or her laugh is heard but she is not seen at all. Another unseen entity knocks over the Christmas tree every year. Others have heard tapping, as if someone is dancing—but when the curious go to investigate, they find no one is there. Objects have fallen over by themselves. Guests in the Burgundy Room have reported seeing an impression on the bed that appears on its own.

CONCLUSION

In this book, you've been introduced to several haunted locations around Northern Virginia. As you can see, many of these locations are accessible to visit. But know that not every location will be open to exploring the paranormal. The stories collected here come from documented cases, interviews and stories passed down throughout different generations. If a location is public property and open to its haunted history, by all means, go out there and have some fun while having meaningful conversations. If a location is private property, respect the boundaries and enjoy the location from a distance. If any of the haunted locations are roads or railroads or on rough terrain, please exercise caution; I don't want you to join this collection of ghost stories in a later edition!

Also, know that the businesses mentioned at the time of this writing may not be at their current locations by the time you visit. Consult the address listed to confirm who is in business.

Finally, you've also learned the histories of the people who lived in Northern Virginia before us. Some came from positions of power and privilege, while others were marginalized, poor, oppressed—the list goes on. Approach and retell these stories knowing that the people behind the lore were real, and they deserve to have their stories told with respect.

Ghost stories continue to generate interest in historic places and landmark events of the past. As long as people still exist, ghostly legends will continue. In fact, today's lived experiences are tomorrow's ghost stories. What story do you want future generations to tell?

Paranormal Glossary

ELECTROMAGNETIC FIELD (EMF)
The electronic energy that comes from computers, televisions, wires, phones and more.

ELECTRONIC VOICE PHENOMENON (EVP)
Voices that can be heard in audio recordings but are often not loud enough for human ears.

ESTES METHOD
The Estes Method—using a spirit box, a blindfold and noise-canceling headphones—is credited to a team of paranormal investigators who first tried the method at the Stanley Hotel in Estes Park, Colorado. The investigator will put on noise-canceling headphones plugged into the spirit box and put on the blindfold, making them the receiver. Someone else, usually in a different room or far enough away that the receiver cannot hear, will ask questions. The receiver will then say out loud what they are either hearing or feeling. It is believed that the Estes Method puts the receiver in a trance, making them more open for spirit communication.

GHOSTTUBE
GhostTube is an app that claims to leverage the user's mobile device's actual sensors to detect fluctuations in the environment. It selects words from a

pre-populated data bank and tracks audio recordings during paranormal investigations. No special sound or visual effects are added—just raw readings from the device. Read more about how GhostTube works at https://ghosttube.com.

GHOSTTUBE SEER

GhostTube Seer is the world's first AI-powered paranormal tool. The app combines theories of spiritual communication and manipulation of environmental sensors with the human psyche, mind and interpretation using the power of modern-day artificial intelligence algorithms.

KII METER

A KII meter detects electromagnetic fields. It has been long speculated that spikes in EMF, read through a KII meter, are indicative of a paranormal presence.

REM-POD

A reactive device that is usually round and has an antenna. When someone or something is close to the antenna, it will start beeping, and lights will illuminate. Should a REM-Pod go off with no one near it, it is believed that this is linked to paranormal activity.

SPIRIT BOX

A radio that sweeps through stations, either forward or backward. The sweeping can be done at a fast or slow rate. It is believed that people can use a spirit box to communicate with ghosts, as their voices will become audible.

BIBLIOGRAPHY

Alexandria (VA) Gazette. "Ben Rubin: Self Confessed Slayer of Eva Roy to Be Examined in Order to Corroborate His Story of Crime." September 21, 1918.

———. "Held for Girl's Death." August 9, 1918.

Alexandria Ghosts. "The Ghosts of Carlyle House." June 2, 2021, https://alexandriaghosts.com.

Allshouse, Frances A.R., and Andrew B. Allshouse. *Ghosts of the Old Jail*. Self-published, Createspace, 2013.

American Battlefield Trust. "Battle of Ball's Bluff Facts & Summary." October 21, 2018. https://www.battlefields.org.

———. "Battle of Second Manassas Facts & Summary." January 14, 2009, https://www.battlefields.org.

Annandale Today. "Annandale History Comes to Life at Oak Hill." October 1, 2013, https://annandaletoday.com.

———. "Oak Hill, Annandale's Oldest House, Welcomes Visitors One Day a Year." October 17, 2010.

Arlington Historical Society. "Ball-Sellers House." April 19, 2016. https://arlingtonhistoricalsociety.org.

Arlington Public Library. "Last Rites for a Funeral Home." June 11, 2012. https://library.arlingtonva.us.

ARLnow.com "Arlington Funeral Home Closes to Make Way for Development." December 28, 2011, https://www.arlnow.com.

———. "Exhibit Explores Rosslyn's Colorful Past (and Bright Future)." February 22, 2011. https://www.arlnow.com.

Atlas Obscura. "Lee Chapel Cemetery." https://www.atlasobscura.com.

Bahr, Jeff, et al. *Weird Virginia*. New York: Sterling, 2007.

Bennett, Cindy L. *Wicked Fairfax County*. Charleston, SC: The History Press, 2018.

Boundary Stones. "Dead Man's Hollow." https://boundarystones.weta.org/.

Boyd, Aila. "Spooky Season Is Year-Round in Virginia. Here Are 5 Ghost/Haunted Tours to Check Out." Dogwood, 8 December 2022. https://vadogwood.com.

Braiker, Brian. "In Leesburg, a Spirited History Tour." *Washington Post*, October 31, 1999, https://www.washingtonpost.com.

Breedan, Morgan. "Preserving Brentsville's History." *Brentsville Neighbors* (September 2015), https://historicprincewilliam.org.

Carlson, Peter. "50 Years Ago, Unidentified Flying Objects from Way Beyond the Beltway Seized the Capital's Imagination." *Washington Post*, July 21, 2002.

Chasing Lost History (blog). "The Remeum." http://chasinglosthistory.blogspot.com.

Christiano, Carla. "Rockledge: An Occoquan Survivor." *Prince William Living* (March 2012): 8–10.

Clark, Charles S. "Finding the Febrey Homestead." *Arlington Historical Magazine* (2015): 7–18.

———. "Our Man in Arlington." *Falls Church News-Press*, April 4, 2012. https://www.fcnp.com.

Clark, Charlie. *Hidden History of Arlington County*. Mount Pleasant, SC: Arcadia Publishing, 2017.

Colonial Ghosts. "Historic Avenel & Weems-Botts Museum." August 15, 2017. https://colonialghosts.com.

———. "25 of the Most Haunted Places in Virginia. "August 15, 2017. https://colonialghosts.com.

Connection Newspapers. "Loudoun's Haunted History." October 24, 2007. http://www.connectionnewspapers.com.

Curtis, Nellie. "History of Occoquan." Historic Prince William, 1993. https://www.historicprincewilliam.org/.

D'Agostino, Matthew. "Flight of the Madisons: Dolley at Minor's Hill." White House Historical Association. https://www.whitehousehistory.org/.

DC Ghosts. "Creepy Tales from Old Alexandria, VA." March 6, 2021. https://dcghosts.com.

DeVito, Carlo. *Mrs. Lee's Rose Garden*. Kennebunkport, ME: Cider Mill Press, 2015.

DeWan, Olivia. "Leesburg's Most Haunted." *County Chronicle*, November 22, 2021. https://countychronicle.org/

Dickey, Colin. *Ghostland: An American History in Haunted Places*. New York: Viking, 2017.

Du Pont Lee, Marguerite. *Virginia Ghosts*. Virginia Book Company, 1966; originally published 1930.

Elton, P.M. *Ghostly Tales of Selected Virginia State Parks*. Adventure Publications, 2015.

Evening Star. "Boys Blame Curiosity for Mausoleum Break-In." March 27, 1956.

Fairfax County Virginia. "Remey Family Mausoleum (Remeum)—Cemeteries." https://www.fairfaxcounty.gov.

Find a Grave. "Col George Michael Swope (1725–1792)." https://www.findagrave.com.

———. "Ella Ann Coffer Hall (1859–1908)." https://www.findagrave.com.

———. "Eva Barbara Sabina Kuhn Swope (1744–1803)." https://www.findagrave.com.

———. "Gertrude Alice James Robey (1883–1966)." https://www.findagrave.com.

Finley, James. "Converse and Drink with the Dead on the Occoquan Spirits Tour." *Northern Virginia Magazine*, October 8, 2021. https://northernvirginiamag.com.

Fractured Fairfax. "Roundtree Park." http://www.fracturedfairfax.com.

GhostQuest.net. "Haunted Locations: Virginia." https://www.ghostquest.net.

Ghosts of DC. "Dead Man's Hollow: A Dark History of Rosslyn and Arlington." May 15, 2014, https://ghostsofdc.org.

———. "Fire and Explosions Threaten to Destroy Rosslyn." January 14, 2014, https://ghostsofdc.org.

———. "Glebe Road: History of Modern Day Arlington County." February 24, 2014, https://ghostsofdc.org.

Glakas, Barbara. "Remembering Herndon's History: The Ghost in Brush Strokes' Salon." *Herndon, VA Patch*, 3 Oct. 2023, patch.com/virginia/herndon/remembering-herndons-history-ghost-brush-strokes-salon.

Green, Mary Margaret. "Destroys Historic Fairfax House: George's Horse Slept Here, 'Ghost'" Haunted It." *Washington Star*.

Greenway Downs. "The Harper House." https://greenwaydowns.org.

Harden, Blaine. "The Mount Vernon Monster." *Washington Post*, May 11, 1979. https://www.washingtonpost.com.

Harrison Eng, Angela. "Offbeat Postscripts: A Haunting at the Overlee Community Center." Offbeat NOVA, August 6, 2021. https://offbeatnova.com.

Haunted Commonwealth (blog). "Haunted Places in Virginia." http://hauntedva.blogspot.com.

Hess, Michael D. *Haunted Clarke County, Virginia*. Mount Pleasant, SC: Arcadia Publishing, 2019.

Hines, Emilee. *Virginia Myths and Legends*. Lanham, MD: Rowman & Littlefield, 2015.

Historical Marker Database. "Colchester Historical Marker." https://www.hmdb.org.

———. "The Huldah Coffer House Historical Marker." https://www.hmdb.org.

———. "The Silas Burke House Historical Marker." https://www.hmdb.org.

HistoricOccoquan.com. "Haunting of Historic Occoquan." https://historicoccoquan.com.

Holland, Sarah. "A Ghostly Education: Living and Learning Folklore through Mason's Legends and Lore." George Mason University, October 31, 2023. https://www.gmu.edu.

Hollmuller, Anne. "And Other Bloody Happenings: Rosslyn and the Dangers of Dead Man's Hollow." Boundary Stones, May 9, 2018. https://boundarystones.weta.org.

Huzzard, David. "Super NoVa Realty by David Huzzard: Ghost Stories of Northern Virginia: Walney Road." *Super NoVa Realty by David Huzzard* (blog), March 13, 2012, http://supernovarealty.blogspot.com.

Inside NoVa. "Demolition of Old Wakefield High School Starts." November 24, 2013. https://www.insidenova.com.

Jackman, Tom. "Arlington House Haunted by Jim Morrison." *Washington Post*, May 11, 2011. https://www.washingtonpost.com.

Jenny's Blog. "The Walney Road Hitchhiker." June 7, 2010. http://jennyluke.blogspot.com.

Jirak, Gianna. "Haunts of Prince William: Read the Legends, Visit the Sites, Learn the History." Inside NoVa, October 31, 2020. https://www.insidenova.com.

Jones, Erica. "A Chill Went Down My Spine: 3 of Alexandria's Spookiest Ghost Stories." NBC4 Washington, October 16, 2017. https://www.nbcwashington.com.

Keen, Michael. "The Falling Ghosts of Carlyle House Historic Park." M.A. Kleen, November 17, 2020. https://michaelkleen.com.

Kelly, John. "What Does a Sarcophagus from Italy Have to Do with a Virginia Mausoleum?" *Washington Post*, February 12, 2019.

Manassas Virginia. "Annaburg." https://www.manassasva.gov.

———. "ARTfactory." https://www.manassasva.gov.

McElhaney, Judy. *Ghost Stories of Woodlawn Plantation*. Epm Publications, 1992.

McMorrow, Michael. "Overlee Clubhouse Is Gone." Connection Newspapers, February 16, 2012. http://www.connectionnewspapers.com.

Memorable Women's Travel (blog). "Four Haunted Houses in Leesburg, Virginia." October 31, 2021, https://memorablewomenstravel.com.

Michaels, Denver. *Strange Tales from Virginia's Mountains: The Norton Woodbooger, the Missing Beale Treasure, the Ghost Town of Lignite and More*. Charleston, SC: The History Press, 2020.

Mills, Andrew L. *Haunted Prince William County*. Mount Pleasant, SC: Arcadia Publishing, 2020.

Mills, Charles A. *Virginia Legends & Lore*. Charleston, SC: The History Press, August 23, 2021.

Nathan. "Lee Chapel Cemetery—Virginia, and the County's Grisliest Murder." RANDOM Times, March 23, 2020. https://random-times.com.

National Park Service. "The Battle of First Manassas (First Bull Run)." 2016. https://www.nps.gov.

Nesbitt, Mark. *Cursed in Virginia*. Lanham, MD: Rowman & Littlefield, 2017.

———. "Ghosts of Gettysburg Haunted Daytrips: Ball's Bluff." Mark Nesbitt, October 5, 2020. https://markvnesbitt.wordpress.com.

———. "Ghosts of Gettysburg Haunted Daytrips: Manassas." Mark Nesbitt, August 13, 2020. https://markvnesbitt.wordpress.com.

Northern Virginia Magazine. "The Creepiest Urban Legends of Northern Virginia." October 24, 2017. https://northernvirginiamag.com.

NOVA Parks. "Carlyle House Historic Park." October 11, 2021, https://www.novaparks.com.

Occoquan Spirits—Haunted Pub Crawl and Ghost Tour. http://occoquanspirits.com.

O'Connell, Michael. "Remembering Herndon's Haunted History: Dead Man's Hollow." Patch, October 4, 2022. https://patch.com.

Old Town Home. "Around Old Town: The Historic 1796 Dr. James Craik House." July 18, 2013. https://www.oldtownhome.com.

Only In Your State. "Stay Overnight in the 169-Year-Old Black Horse Inn, an Allegedly Haunted Spot in Virginia." September 21, 2019. https://www.onlyinyourstate.com.

Pekow, Charles. "The Historic Annaburg Manor Is Being Rehabilitated, but Its Future Is Still Uncertain." *Northern Virginia Magazine*, January 3, 2023. https://northernvirginiamag.com.

Peters, Laura. "Ghosts of Leesburg Highlighted in Hauntings Tour." *Loudoun (VA) Times-Mirror*, October 15, 2011, https://www.loudountimes.com.

Phelan, Bob. "Antiques Roadshow." PBS, May 18, 2015. https://www.pbs.org.

Pope, Michael Lee. *Ghosts of Alexandria*. Mount Pleasant, SC: Arcadia Publishing, 2010.

———. *Wicked Northern Virginia*. Mount Pleasant, SC: Arcadia Publishing, 2014.

Powell, Lewis O., IV. "Reappearance of the Suave Zouaves—Manassas, Virginia." *Southern Spirit Guide* (blog), September 13, 2022. https://www.southernspiritguide.org.

Prince William Living. "Is There a Spectre Haunting Occoquan?" October 12, 2020. https://princewilliamliving.com.

Pruntel, Alison. "Local History: Fauquier County Ghosts." Fauquier Public Library, October 17, 2017. https://www.fauquierlibrary.org.

Pugh, Kari. "Rippon Lodge: "Ghostly and Sinister."" Inside NoVa, October 31, 2014. https://www.insidenova.com.

Pyzyk, Katie. "Then and Now: Virginia Hardware in Rosslyn." ARLnow.com, July 31, 2012. https://www.arlnow.com.

———. "Workers Report Ghost Sightings at Overlee." ARLnow.com. https://www.arlnow.com.

Reddit. "Has Anyone Heard of (or Seen) the Ghost of Eva Roy?" November 1, 2014. https://www.reddit.com/r/nova/.

Richmond (VA) Times-Dispatch. "Plan to Exhume Body of Murdered Eva Roy." August 15, 1918.

Roberts, Jay. "Ghost on the Occoquan: A Look at Colchester." *Jaybird's Jottings*, January 7, 2014. https://jay.typepad.com.

Robison, Debbie. *Minor's Hill House.* Fairfax County History Commission, August 30, 2016.

———. "Truth or Myth: The Legend of Miss Ann and Captain Hawkins Oak Hill, Fairfax County, Virginia." Northern Virginia History Notes, December 18, 2014. http://www.novahistory.org.

Roos, Dave. "When UFOs Buzzed the White House and the Air Force Blamed the Weather." History, August 24, 2023. https://www.history.com.

Rosenwald, Michael S. "How UFO Sightings Went from Joke to National Security Worry in Washington." *Washington Post*, May 23, 2021. https://www.washingtonpost.com.

Rosslyn Business Improvement District. "Rosslyn's History." https://www.rosslynva.org.

Sadler, Tierney. "Haunted Places & Urban Legends of Fairfax County." Fairfax County, Virginia, October 3, 2023. http://www.fxva.com.

Sandlin, Claudia. "Ghosts March through Time at Battlefield, Legend Says." *Washington Post*, October 26, 1989.

Saulny, Susan. "The Ghosts of Leesburg's Past." *Washington Post*, October 26, 1997. https://www.washingtonpost.com.

Scheel, Eugene. "Timeline of Important African American Events in Loudoun County, Virginia." History of Loudoun County, Virginia. http://www.loudounhistory.org.

Schlosser, S.E. *Spooky Virginia*. Lanham, MD: Rowman & Littlefield, 2023.

Schwartz, Susan. *Haunted Inns and Hotels of Virginia*. Mount Pleasant, SC: Arcadia Publishing, 2023.

Shackelford, Susanne. *Mrs. Robey: Notes for Presentation at Fall Fundraiser Tea at the Library*. October 14, 2006.

Shea, Daniel. "Historic Home Burns Down." *Globe*, January 8, 1978.

Smith, J.J. *Haunted Alexandria and Northern Virginia*. Schiffer, 2009.

Solano, Sophia. "1787 House for Sale in Alexandria, Va., for Nearly $5 Million." *Washington Post*, June 2, 2023. https://www.washingtonpost.com.

Taylor, Dan "Remembering Herndon's History: Haunted Herndon." Patch, October 4, 2017. https://patch.com.

Taylor, L.B., Jr. *The Big Book of Virginia Ghost Stories*. Stackpole Books, 2010.

———. *Haunted Virginia*. Stackpole Books, 2009.

Thompson, David W. *Haunted Potomac River Valley*. Mount Pleasant, SC: Arcadia Publishing, 2021.

Tipple, Stephanie. "A Dumfries House Full of History, and Chilling Experiences." Potomac Local News, October 31, 2012. https://www.potomaclocal.com.

Town of Leesburg, Virginia. "A Brief History of Leesburg." https://www.leesburgva.gov.

U.S. Ghost Adventures. "The Haunted Aquia Church." January 18, 2023. https://usghostadventures.com.

Virginia Haunted Houses. "Bunny Man Bridge." https://www.virginiahauntedhouses.com.

Visit Loudoun. "Harrison Hall." https://www.visitloudoun.org.

———. "Leesburg Ghost Tours." https://www.visitloudoun.org.

Walker, Jordan. "Rediscover Haunted Arlington." Arlington Public Library, October 28, 2019. https://library.arlingtonva.us.

Walker, Steve. "Research Center Guides: Local History: The Bunny Man Unmasked." Fairfax County Virginia. https://research.fairfaxcounty.gov.

Washington Post. "Mrs. Remey's Death Held Suicide." August 5, 1932.

Whelan, Aubrey. "Ghost of Girl Appears, Construction Worker Flees." ConstructionEquipmentGuide.com, October 31, 2017. https://www.constructionequipmentguide.com.

White, Amy Brecount. "Poltergeist Problems." *Arlington Magazine*, May 16, 2013. https://www.arlingtonmagazine.com.

Woodville (MS) Republican. "Couldn't Scare Prisoner with Man-Made 'Spook.'" November 9, 1918.

Wosahla, Steve. "Bluegrass in Brentsville, History Around Us & the Ghost of Jimmy Martin." No Depression, September 29, 2015. https://www.nodepression.com.

About the Author

Alex Matsuo is a paranormal researcher, investigator and author. She is the founder of the Association of Paranormal Study and runs the blog *The Spooky Stuff*, which features various paranormal topics and historical places with reports of ghosts. Alex has been featured on Travel Channel, Discovery Plus, CTV Sci-Fi and Tubi. Some of her other books include *Women of the Paranormal Volume 1: A Brief History*, *The Hamptonville Hauntings: Ghosts of the Trivette Clinic*, *One Bed Over: A Hospital Haunting* and *The Brave Mortal's Guide to Ghost Hunting*. Alex holds a master of arts in theater from San Diego State University and works as a learning experience designer in Arlington, Virginia.